365-Days of Knowing Who You Are in Christ Jesus

&

Devotional Journal

by

Carol Babalola

A Publication by

Fate Academy Publisher Ltd

Romford

London

fateacadmy.org@gmail.com

We offer Significant discounts to authors or organisations who are interested in purchasing bulk quantities of Fate Academy's books.

Please contact us at via email addresses below:

fateacademy.org@gmail.com

fatexclusive@yahoo.com

All rights reserved.

Printed In the United Kingdom (England, UK)

ISBN Number

978-1-64764-228-0

This Journal Belongs To: ....

From: ....

Date: ....

Selah!

"Selah" is a word that will appear frequently in this journal publication. It simply means 'to pause' or 'to reflect'. It is a request for the reader or listener to pause, think, meditate, and reflect on what has just been said or read.

****

❧ Dedication ❧

I dedicate this book to God Almighty, the creator of Heaven and Earth, Jesus Christ the Son, and the Holy Spirit, my Helper.

To my children who continually stand by me through thick and thin.

To all the children, the youth, adolescents, and adults out there… who are longing to know who they are in Christ Jesus.

For those who are anxious, overwhelmed, frustrated, tired, and perhaps depressed, because of identity crises in the absence of understanding their identity.

May You Find Grace To Discover, Who You Are In Christ Jesus.

I Love You All, With The Love Of God.

MCB

Minister Carol Babalola.

✨ Foreword ✨

One of the lost disciplines of our faith walk today is the place of personal morning devotion and what we call "quiet time" because a lot of people have become cold, lukewarm and nonchalant about developing their personal walk with God.

We have become filled with activity and busyness that we have lost sight of what really matters, not realising that activity is a killer of sensitivity.

We have made prayer and communication with God a last resort instead of our first resource, and have ended up as victims instead of victors.

We have abandoned the place of discipleship and settled for shallowness and lack of depth of understanding, and this has raised a generation of believers that can't walk in dominion and represent God well as kingdom ambassadors.

Online prayer platforms has become a fig leave and crutch for many, and have replaced their personal time with God.

One major aspect of my own personal growth for the last 36 years has been my daily morning devotion with God, and the use of devotionals because I am first of all a child of God that needs to grow my relationship with my father.

I began with every day with Jesus by Selwyn Hughes in the late 80s , and later started using our daily bread because of my kids to help them with local content when they were younger, until year 2001 when I discovered open heavens by pastor Adeboye and till date that's what we use as a family.

It's 4.03am here now, and I am awake writing this forward on my devotional desk with worship song playing after which I will go into the devotional in front of me now and bible Reading and wrap up with prayers.

I have shared all this with you so you know the importance of a devotional like this one and maximize the opportunity it brings.

The author has done an amazing job by focusing on one major aspect of life that needs attention if we are going to maximize our possibilities in life and become the best version of ourselves- our identity.

Ignorance of who we are and our identity in Christ has given room to identity crises, inferiority complex, low self-esteem and gender confusion in our world today, and glory be to God for a specialised devotional like this that has made the issue of identity a focus for a whole year.

Congrats to the author for this great and amazing contribution to the development of humanity.

I recommend this devotional to anyone that is tired of playing church and doing religion but is ready to go deeper in their walk with God.

Welcome to an adventure in the spirit and may the lord perfect all that concerns you and yours.

> Keep your dream alive and keep the fire burning.
>
> Yours for the kingdom
>
> Olumide Emmanuel
>
> Overseer over the truth of Calvary ministries and her network of churches globally.
>
> author and global speaker.
>
> An apostle in the marketplace.

Contents

Preface 1

Introduction 4

Chapter 1 9

My Identity and Who I am In Christ. 9

Chapter 2 17

Our Inheritance and Rights As A Child Of God 17

Chapter 3 26

Discovering our Significance and Worth 26

Chapter 4 33

Discovering Who You are 33

Chapter 5 50

In Search of Significance: 50

Discovering Meaning and Purpose in Life 50

Chapter 6 58

Understanding What Defines Our worth 58

Chapter 7 65

Your Identity - Chosen by God. 65

Daily Devotional And Journaling 68

Review 373

Establishing Foundations – through Self-Esteem 373

Memorise And Meditate On These Scriptures 378

Index 385

Preface

Do you Know Who You Are in Christ? What a Question, one would wonder…!

Hello Dearest Ambassadors of the Highest God and the light of the world.

I want to let you know that you are a *phenomenally uniquely unique being* and significant!

Perhaps, you may have forgotten, If so... I am here if you please allow me, to remind you.

You are God's masterpiece, His workmanship created in Christ Jesus to do His good works.

You are the apple of God's eye, and you are complete in Christ Jesus, who is the head of all principality and power.

You are a chosen generation, Royal priesthood, and you are called to rule and reign on the earth as king and queen/princess.

You are loved, adopted, redeemed, and set apart for His glory, and you are an ambassador of the kingdom of God.

Don't you ever behave like your past experiences or your current challenges…

The devil wants you to think that you are not useful, not beautiful, not smart enough, that you are the cause of your struggle, or your struggle is who you are, but none of these is true, it is a lie from the pit of hell.

You have been redeemed and bought at a price which is the blood of Jesus. You are what God says you are, your history, issues, anxiety, depression, anger, resentment, unforgiveness, bitterness, or frustration do not and will NEVER determine who you are in Christ.

I have always wanted to write about identity in Christ Jesus, since I wrote my first book, Who Are You, ten years ago. But the cares and challenges of this world had prevented me from birthing this precious gift until now. The writing of this journal came about when my last child asked me to get her a devotional journal with bible references, and at the same time, I noticed that most people, especially her age group, were struggling with identity crises.

I asked God what He would like me to do as a solution to this problem, and then I was prompted by the Holy Spirit to write a Devotional Journal, and a workbook as a sequel to my previous book, *Who Are You*.

At such a time as this, God is looking for solution providers in the kingdom to bring emotional healing, teachers on identity crises, low self-esteem, and limiting beliefs because all the solution is in Christ Jesus, and He wants us to live abundant life, and to prosper in every area of your life. John 10:10, & 3 John 1:2.

I pray that this journal will provide you with the solutions that you need to know, who you are in Christ, your rights as a child of God, and to strengthen your faith and walk with God, no matter the season of life, you may be now. God promises never to leave nor forsake you, and whatever the enemy meant for evil, he is turning it around for your good.

I hope and pray that as you record your thoughts, prayers, reflections, applications, and desires, you will look back to count all the blessings that God has given in your life over the years. Thank you very much for allowing me to be a part of your journey of knowing who you are in Christ Jesus. May the Lord bless you and keep you; may the Lord make his face shine upon you and be gracious to you, and may the Lord lift his countenance upon you and give you peace as you embark on this journey.

MCB

Carol Babalola.

Introduction

Identity is defined as: the qualities, beliefs, personality traits, appearance, and/or expressions that characterise a person or a group. Identity emerges during childhood as children start to comprehend their self-concept, and it remains a consistent aspect throughout different stages of life. (Wikipedia, September 2023)

or

The distinguishing character, the personality of an individual, or the relation established by spiritual or psychological identification and the condition of being the same with something described or asserted defines identity.

"As a Believer, you are secured by the supernatural glue of the Trinity. So, to be separated from Christ would require prying open the hand of the Father (John 10:29), and being snatched from the Son, after breaking the seal of the Holy Spirit". (Ephesians. 1:13-14)

Jesus became one of us so that we could become one of His, through His death and resurrection. As you accept Jesus as your lord and saviour, God did more than forgiveness of your sins. He made you a member of His family (Ephesians 2:19). And as a new-born baby arrives with a permanent genetic code that is theirs, every spiritually born-again person will also receive a Spiritual genetic code. (2 Corinthians 5:17)

As you accept Christ and bond yourself to Him through faith, you become a new creation with all your past sins forgiven, you now have guidance and nurture for your present life and security with hope for your future. Selah!

Now as a born-again, you have access to all that Jesus Christ is and have become a joint heir to God the Father, and as he is in all His attributes, so are we in this world (1 John 4:17). God loves and hears you as He does to Jesus (Romans 8:39)

In a nutshell, identity in Christ means every child of God can point to Jesus, and before the Father's throne, testify: "I am with him. (Selah)!!!

Before you know who, you are, you must be able to identify your source, which is God. You possess his nature and likeness, and the word of God has made you understand that you are his child, His reflection, His workmanship, and masterpiece. You are awesome, a walking miracle with greatness inside of you. He has created you a new in Christ Jesus, so you can do the things He planned for you long before time ago. (Ephesians 2:10) spelled it out, now you Gentiles are no longer strangers or foreigners you are citizens along with all of God's holy people, you are a member of His family. What an awesome and lovely Father you have, who out of his own will decided to make you, his child.

As you are getting to know who you are. It will be a witness for you and speak on your behalf just as our Lord Jesus Christ did when he said that He is the light of the world. And that He knows where He was going and where He came from, (John 8:12-14 NLT), and He was very confident about who he was, and not afraid to say so, you can do the same today.

Jesus was very emphatic about His identity in this passage, so you should be when others try to define who you are or when you are confused and comparing yourself with others. Jesus said if you follow Him, you will not walk in darkness because you will have the light to lead you in your darkest hours, which is when you go through the water of life, it will not overflow you and through the fire, you shall not be burned. "

"But now, God's Message, the God who made you in the first place, Jacob, the One who got you started, Israel: *"Don't be afraid, I've redeemed you. I've called your name. You're mine.*

His promises offer safety: *"When you're in over your head, I'll be there with you. When you're in rough waters, you will not go down.*

Isaiah 43:2 - MSG - When you're in over your head, I'll be there with ...

When you're between a rock and a hard place, it won't be a dead end. Because I am God, your personal God, The Holy of Israel, your Saviour. I paid a huge price for you: all of Egypt, with rich Cush and Seba thrown in! *That's* how much you mean to me! *That's* how much I love you!

I would sell off the whole world to get you back or trade the creation just for you (Isaiah 43:2 MSG)" You are inscribed in the palm of God's hands, bought with the incorruptible blood of Jesus, and as soon as you become born again, your bloodline changes to that of Jesus Christ (Royalty bloodline).

As a result of what Jesus has done for you, you are to raise your confidence and boldness in Christ like Stephen, who testified of the truth so boldly that wicked men stoned him to death (Acts 6:7). Therefore, do not allow anything to intimidate you anymore.

The Bible says, "*They that know their God shall be strong and do great exploits.*" When you know who you are in Christ and whose you belong to, you can do great exploits in your area of influence and take your rightful place with authority. Good things come to those who know their identity in Christ. When you find yourself questioning your value, worth, looks, ability, or looking outward for reinforcement, stop and think about the strength of God that lies within you. "He that is within you is greater than that in the world. "*You, dear children, are from God and have overcome them because the one who is in you is greater than the one who is in the world.* (1 John 4:

This book will help to save you, from pain, frustration, and confusion in your walk with the Lord Jesus Christ and, will help you to discover who you are and to be passionate about helping others to discover their identity in Christ as well. (Selah)

God never promised you a trouble-free life. In fact, He forewarned you that in this world, there will be tribulations, but be of good cheer, that; I have overcome the world" (John 16:33) This is the hope you have in Christ Jesus. (Selah)

Embracing Mindfulness and Gratitude

Mindfulness and gratitude foster a deeper appreciation for the present moment and the blessings in our lives. Engaging in practices such as meditation or journaling can help us uncover hidden layers of significance. The ability to be fully present and cultivate a sense of gratitude for life's experiences enables a profound connection to the world and reveals the underlying significance of each moment.

Chapter 1

My Identity and Who I am In Christ.

Identity Crises

An identity crisis can be described as a time of despair, uncertainty, frustration, confusion, not knowing who you are, and many more in a person's life. This period of crisis usually occurs when a person's sense of identity becomes insecure, unclear about a change in life, and unstable circumstances, due to upbringing, peer pressure, job, from society, friends, and the primary caregivers. From birth we begin the search to satisfy some inner, unexplainable longing or yearning, this hunger causes us to search for people who will love us, strive for success, feeding our bodies and neglecting our mind and soul, our desire for acceptance makes us to perform to gain praise from others and looking for others to appreciate us for our sacrifices. Anyone who live for the love and attention of others is never satisfied but having a sign of an identity crises. The desire to be loved and accepted is a symptom of a deeper need and if the need is not curb, it will be a source of our emotional pain and worthlessness.

An identity crisis can happen at any time of life.

How to tell if you are having identity crises and Symptoms of identity crisis.

There are some common symptoms of identity crises, which are low self-esteem, feeling lost or aimless, not having a sense of purpose or understanding your values, questioning who you are, your value or worth, beliefs, passions, self-neglect, having suicidal thoughts, emotional imbalance, feeling insecure, anxiety, panic attacks, sexual identity, depression, and others.

How can an identity crisis lead to the symptoms mentioned above?

Research has found that identity crises are prevalent in people with mental health issues, negative self-views, and when the way you define yourself suffers. If you are struggling with an identity crisis, and or experiencing feelings of hopelessness, doubting your sexuality, worthlessness, or loss of interest in things once enjoyed, fatigue, irritability, changes in appetite, or weight, difficulty in concentrating, being not motivated, low energy and finding it hard to sleep. And if you are having any of these symptoms, please seek for help from a trained health professional or talk to your doctor.

How to cope with an identity crisis when you do not know who you are.

If you are confused and struggling with identity crises, you are not alone. Many of us are going through the same issue while others have passed through that stage in life.

The first step is to ground yourself in your core values and figure out how this is important to you. If you are a Christian, your core value is your beliefs, to love God and others, (1 John 4:19), to be courageous (Joshua 1:9), be generous (proverbs 22:9) , respect all (1 Peter 2:17) the value of hope is confident expectation, it is an assurance in God, (Proverbs 23:18), to have peace of mind and be peaceable with others, (Romans 14:19).

A Christian is someone who reflect the characterises of Christ. Let me tell you, many of us Christians today are experiencing eclipse in our lives, because you do not know who you are, as the light of the world, when light comes, darkness disappears.

This is the reason why, we are not reflecting the sun, Jesus Christ our source.

If you do not reflect Jesus, there's no way others will see Him through you and be the light that they are called to be in the world.

God placed you where you are today to be the light there, to win souls for the Kingdom of God through your behaviour, character, attitude, and good works.

And you must be intentional in applying Christian's value daily. Paul says, "Whatever you have learned or received or heard from me or seen in me—put it into practice. And the God of peace will be with you" (Philippians 4:9). The more you read the word of God, the better you know Him and understand His purpose for you in the world. When you become intimate with the Holy Spirit, He teaches you to value what God holds dear and grow to love these values as well, only then would you lead others to eternal life through Jesus Christ. The way you love and treat others defines your Christian values,

"[Let your] love be sincere (a real thing); hate what is evil [loathe all ungodliness, turn in horror from wickedness], but hold fast to that which is good.

12:10 Love one another with brotherly affection [as members of one family], giving precedence {and} showing honour to one another. (Romans 12:9 AMP)

The bible says that you are fearfully and wonderfully made, (psalm139:13-14), so, get to know yourself through the eye of God that you are complete in Him who is the head of all principality and power. God chose you, know that you are valuable to God and uniquely made for His purpose.

The next step is to redefine what value is most important to you, no matter what stage you are, ask yourself questions:

- What value do I care about? Why do I care about it?
- What is the *yearning* of your soul calling out for?

Then look for a quiet place to reflect, mediate on what God said about you. In knowing who you are, you Must be aware of your emotions, and you are allowed to feel your emotions and afterwards seek for support and help from professionals. You can go on a retreat or somewhere quiet alone to learn more about who you are without the pressure from outside and influence from others.

Deal with your mental fitness by having a sound mind, think about good things, for your personal victory in any situation.

Philippians 4:8 *Finally, brother and sisters, whatever is true, whatever is noble, whatever is right, pure, lovely, admirable, if anything is excellent or praiseworthy, think about such things.*

You can start journaling your most impactful memories, beautiful things that had happened in the past, be thankful about life because a living dog is better than a dead lion. The Holy Spirit is our counsellor and comforter, so spend more time with Him alone, and He shall reveal the secret answers to your questions to you and you will have more clarity for your life. Do not dare to give up, no matter how long a tunnel is, there is

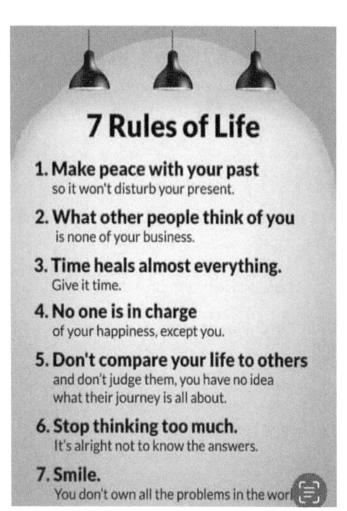

7 Rules of Life

1. **Make peace with your past** so it won't disturb your present.
2. **What other people think of you** is none of your business.
3. **Time heals almost everything.** Give it time.
4. **No one is in charge** of your happiness, except you.
5. **Don't compare your life to others** and don't judge them, you have no idea what their journey is all about.
6. **Stop thinking too much.** It's alright not to know the answers.
7. **Smile.** You don't own all the problems in the worl

always light at the end of the tunnel. Do not limit yourself, you are much more than you think, there is so much untapped potentials within you, go out for new experiences then learn, unlearn, and relearn for the sky is not your limit, because the sky is limitless!!! you are limitless, and free to be the best of who you really are. Selah!

Arise! Shine, let the world see your good works and glorify your Father in heaven. (Mathew5:16)

According to Psychologist Erik Erikson who studied identity and the concept of the identity crisis, in his theory, he found that there are eight different developmental stages of identity. He believed that the period of adolescence played a particularly vital role in the formation of a person's identity.

He described this stage of life as one of "identity vs. role confusion" and believed that people who can commit to a strong identity grows up with a solid sense of self, while those who struggle with who they are, develop identity crises later in life.

At each stage he captured different virtues, and they are as follows:

What Psychologist says about you.

- Basic trust vs. Mistrust
- Autonomy vs. shame and doubt
- Initiative vs guilt
- Industry vs inferiority
- Identity vs. role confusion
- Intimacy vs Isolation
- Generativity Vs. Stagnation
- Ego integrity vs. despair

Individuation: Is the process by which an individual becomes uniquely different (distinct). *Individuation* distinguishes you from everybody else, which means that you are unique, exceptional and a masterpiece. (Carl Jung.) Individuation involved becoming your own person, with your own beliefs and ideals that might be separate from those of your parents and society. Individuation is a lifelong process involving all the choices that make you uniquely yourself.

(Carl Jung.) The society and family influence and plays important role in identity. A person is challenged when an aspect of their identity does not align with the expectations of the environment or society.

What God says about you and your rights as a child of God.

While Psychology focus on self-worth with a goal of simply feeling good about yourself, and all about self without the help of God. However, the biblical self-concept goes far beyond limited perspective. The truth is that our worth is based on the perception of ourselves, God, and the word of God. When it comes to self-esteem or self-worth, it is the feeling of significance that is crucial to a man's emotional, spiritual, and social stability and is the driving force within the human spirit.

To understand this need in our life, opens the door to understand the way we act and do things (actions and attitudes) if not we will be chasing shadows, wasting time and money searching for love, acceptance, and success without understanding the need that compels us. We must come to realisation that this hunger is God given and can only be satisfied by Him only. Our value is not based or dependant on the acceptance of other people, rather the source for our love and acceptance is in God, our creator, who is love Himself. He is the only one that can fulfil the need that we crave for in other material things.

As a born-again believer, a child of God, a redeemer who has accepted Christ as their saviour and repented of their former sinful ways, you have many rights, gifts, and privileges that comes with salvation as a package. Your inheritance as a child of God is too numerous to count. God the Father, Son and the Holy Spirit are one and He want a relationship with us, through the sacrifice of Jesus on the cross for us. We can now come boldly to the throne of grace because of what Jesus had done for us. (Hebrews 4:16 NKJV) and you can communicate with God through prayer and the Holy Spirit that dwells within us.

What a great privilege? (Selah). As you a family of God, you have the right to use the name of Jesus Christ, the blood of Jesus, and you can pray in the name of Jesus and our Heavenly father will answer you. Jesus's righteousness (right standing with God is yours as well). You have the right to always triumph. (2Corinthians 2:14), you have the right to resist the devil and he will flee from you (James 4:7

You are the one to enforce your right as a child of God to defeat the devil by speaking the Word of God in faith. The word of God is yeah and Amen, powerful and sharper than any two-edged sword, act on His Word now and expect a result. God said to the Israelites, 'As I live,' says the LORD, 'just what you have spoken in My hearing I will most certainly do to you" (Numbers 14:28).

Always speak triumph and victory over every situation, challenges, or circumstances in your life, according to His promises, for your life. Never give up, keep speaking, believe in it and do not doubt the word, for it may tarry, but it will surely come to pass. David said "I will say of the Lord, He is my refuge and my fortress" it is when you say by speaking the word that the answer comes.

Chapter 2

Our Inheritance and Rights As A Child Of God

1: You have the right to be free.

"Therefore, if the Son makes you free, you shall be free indeed." –John 8:36 (NKJV)

Having been created by God, He gave you different gifts of life, like dominion and free will to be able to live this life victoriously.

One might ask, why would God give you free will, and not force you to be righteous? Because God is not a man neither are you robots nor slaves.

He chose you to be His child and a member of His family, the reason why you have the rights, the privileges and the power of choice has been given to man. You have the choice to decide your eternity, the right to choose life or death, blessing or cursing, heaven or hell, and God will never deny you of your choice but still you have the right of freedom.

It is your Choice; God Will Not Force You.

Sometimes, Satan would try to deceive you like he did to Eve at the garden of Eden, that you cannot choose to be free in Christ. And this is a lie from the pit of hell that you are condemned, sick, addicted, depressed, poor, alcoholic, that you cannot change, not righteous, nor forgiven, you should be feeling guilty, and ashamed about your past or whatever you have done wrong.

The truth is that the son Jesus has set you free and you are free indeed, the moment you accept Jesus as your lord and saviour, your sins are forgiven, you start on a clean, clear slate, free from past mistakes, guilt, shame, addiction, prostitution, pornography, depression, anxiety, anger, low self-esteem, and worthlessness. It might be that you feel stuck, thus being symbolically *locked up in the prison…* of lies, guilt and shame. God promise says that there is a key of David that opens all doors, use it to unlock that door now by the blood of Jesus and walk out into the freedom and victory of Christ.

2: You have the right to be healed because by His stipes you are healed.

"By His stripes we are healed." –Isaiah 53:5 (NKJV)

Healing is the children" bread. Jesus has already dealt with that, so do not struggle about this. The bible says, *"Beloved friend, I pray that* **you** *are prospering in every way and that* you *continually enjoy* good health*, just as your soul is prospering."* 3 John 1:2 TPT

3: You Have the Right to Prosper

"And God will generously provide all you need. Then you will always have everything you need, and plenty left over to share with others." 2 Corinthians 9:8

4: You Have the Right to Never Fear Again

"For you did not receive the spirit of bondage again to fear, but you received the Spirit of adoption by whom we cry out, 'Abba, Father.'" –Romans 8:15 (NKJV)

And you did not receive the "spirit of religious duty," leading you back into the fear of never being good enough. But you have received the "Spirit of full acceptance," enfolding you into the family of God. And you will never feel orphaned, for as he rises within us, our spirits join him in saying the words of tender affection, "Beloved Father!" Romans 8:15 TPT

5: You Have the Right to Have Peace

"The Lord will bless His people with peace." –Psalm 29:11 (NASB)

You will keep **in** perfect peace all who trust in you, all whose thoughts are fixed on you! Trust in the Lord Always, For the Lord God Is the Eternal. Isaiah 26:3 TPT. And Perfect peace is complete peace and is guaranteed when we focus on Jesus.

6: You Have the Right to Use the Name of Jesus

"And this is his command: to believe in the name of his Son, Jesus Christ." 1 John 3:23, NIV

7: You Have the Right to Always Triumph

Now thanks be to God who always leads us in triumph in Christ, and through us diffuses the fragrance of His knowledge in every place. 2 Corinthians 2:14

8: You have the right to resist the devil and he will flee from you (James 4:7)

You have the right to resist Satan and to expect him to flee, in all things. And in every area of your life.

9: You have the right to the Grace of God.

But we who live by the Spirit as we eagerly wait to receive by faith the righteousness which God has promised to us. For when we place our faith in Christ Jesus, there is no benefit in being circumcised or being uncircumcised. What is important is faith expressing itself in love. (Galatians 5:5-6)

But the Holy Spirit produces this kind of fruit in our lives: love, joy, peace, patience, kindness, goodness, faithfulness, gentleness, and self-control. There is no law against these things! (22-23, NLT)

10: Those who belong to Christ Jesus have nailed their passions and desires of their sinful nature to His cross and crucified them there.

Since we are living by the Spirit, let us follow the Spirit's leading in every part of our lives. (Galatians 5:22-25)

11: Our parents corrected us for the short time of our childhood as it seemed good to them. But God corrects us throughout our lives for our own good, giving us an invitation to share His holiness. (Hebrews 12:10 TPT)

12: So, let God work His will in you.

Yell a loud *no* to the Devil and watch him make himself scarce. Say a quiet *yes* to God and he'll be there in no time. Quit dabbling in sin. Purify your inner life. Quit playing the field. Hit rock bottom and cry your eyes out. The fun and games are over. Get serious, do get serious to allow God to work in you. Get down on your knees before the Master; it's the only way you'll get on your feet. (James 4:7)

13: The Prodigal Returns Home: Luke 15:20 TPT

"So, the young son set off for home. From a long distance away, his father saw him coming, dressed as a beggar, and great compassion swelled up in his heart for his son who was returning home. The father raced out to meet him, swept him up in his arms, hugged him dearly, and kissed him over and over with tender love.

14: *"I have been crucified with Christ and I no longer live, but Christ lives in me. The life I now live in the body, I live by faith in the Son of God, who loved me and gave himself for me."* Galatians 2:20, NIV

15: **I am freed from pride**.

Philippians 2:3-4 TPT says: *Be free from pride-filled opinions, for they will only harm your cherished unity. Don't allow self-promotion to hide in your hearts, but in authentic humility put others first and view others as more important than yourselves. Abandon every display of selfishness.*

16: In Luke 18:16 TPT we read this:

Seeing what was happening, Jesus called for parents, the children, and his disciples to come and listen to him. Then He told them, "Never hinder a child from coming to me but let them all come, for God's Kingdom belongs to them as much as it does to anyone else. These children demonstrate to you what faith is all about.

17: 1 John 1:9 says when we confess our sins, he forgives us and purifies us. This means we do not need to let shame and guilt control us. Rather, we can embrace forgiveness and our identity and worth in Christ.

18: For I know the thoughts that I think toward you, says the Lord, thoughts of peace and not of evil, to give you a future and a hope. (Jeremiah 29:11 NKJV)

I am reconciled to God, in Harmony with him. (Romans 5:10)

19: And Jesus came and said to them, *"All authority in heaven and on earth has been given to me. Go therefore and make disciples of all nations, baptizing them in the name of the Father and of the Son and of the Holy Spirit."* - Matthew 28:18-19

20: I hear God's Voice: Jesus said, *"**My sheep hear my voice, and I know them, and they follow me**. I give them eternal life, and they will never perish, and no one will snatch them out of my hand."* – John 10:27-28

21: *"But as many as received Him, to them gave the power to become children of God, even to them that believe on His name" (John 1:12).*

Have you, or someone you know ever experienced the goodness, mercy, faithfulness, assurance, and joy of being a part of the family of God? Are you sure of your relationship with God as your Father, the Son, and the Holy Spirit? And are you adhering to your obligation as an obedient child to God? You can enjoy the rights, privileges, blessings, and more for being a child of God, when you are committed to fear God and do the will of God for your life.

Jesus explained, *"I am the Way, I am the Truth, and I am the Life. No one comes next to the Father, except through union with me. To know me is to know my Father too.* John 14:6, TPT.

Are you willing to follow Jesus Christ into the glorious experience of being His brother or sister? It will be the wisest and the most amazing decision that you have ever made, and you will be most grateful to God for taking the right step.

Jesus never promised us a smooth path or an easy journey of life, but He promised never to leave nor forsake us, we were given the greatest victory by God over suffering, sin, and death so that the eternal glory will be much greater compared to the glory of this world.

*I have told you these things, so that in Me you may have [perfect] peace. In the world you have tribulation and distress and suffering, but be courageous [be confident, be undaunted, be filled with joy]; I have overcome the world." [My conquest is accompl*ished, My victory abiding. (John16:33 AMP)

Bad things do happen to good and evil people, just as the sun shines upon the just and unjust, and rain falls on both as well. (Mathew 5:45)

We know that terrible things happened to Jesus, the Son of God. But the Lord promised His children who believes and trust in Christ victory.

As you have known your rights as a child of God, you can walk in that freedom, liberty, victory, healing, authority, goodness, and divine abundance of God. You are no longer a slave to fear because God has not given you the spirit of fear but of power, love, and a sound mind. (2 Timothy 1:7)

Do not fear again, be courageous, you have perfect peace in Christ because your mind stays on Him, you can use the Name of Jesus anytime/anywhere, and you can triumph every day for the rest of your life. Knowing your rights is the first step to taking back everything that belongs to you., that the enemy has stolen from you, or lost in the journey of life, and restoration. You are victorious in Christ Jesus.

New Beginnings

"When a woman who had lived a sinful life in that town learned that Jesus was eating at the Pharisee's house, she brought an alabaster jar of perfume, and as she stood behind Him, at His feet weeping, she began to wet His feet with her tears. Then she wiped them with her hair, kissed them and poured perfume on them." (Luke 7:37,38).

This woman had lived an imperfect life. She had a bad reputation, was rejected by others, stigmatised, and living with shame, but she found the One who would not reject, deny, or shame her. Jesus would save her, give her new hope and a new life.

The Power of Faith. She believed in the greater power of Jesus Christ who can take a mess and turn into a miracle, turn her shame into a testimony, paralyse and drive out her fears, give her honour and new chance in life. The religious leaders judged and condemned her, but Jesus recognised and exalted her, showed her love and kindness.

The Power of Decision. She decided to change her life with the power of God. She put blinders on to the glares and harsh judgements of people. She put in ear plugs to shut out negative comments. Her focus was on only Jesus, the hope of her salvation. You can do the same today, to focus on Christ the solid rock, who will never judge or condemned you.

The Power for Change. Faith in the words of Jesus changed her to change her world. Her new life began that day, "Jesus said to the woman, 'Your faith has saved you; go in peace.'" (Luke 7:50). Your faith in the word of God can bring change to your life and also, change your world as well.

Kingdom Declaration:

Every day is a new day of possibilities because Jesus Christ is the Saviour of all, Lord and my King of all kings.

Chapter 3

Discovering our Significance and Worth

Why is identity important?

In life, identity serves a purpose that can help you live, have a sense of belongingness, define who you are, and for you to take your place in society or community without being insecure, and having low self-esteem. Identity is very crucial for social connections and your well-being because it is tied to other areas of life, like religion, politics, self-worth, values, culture, and languages.

Identity is formed or shaped by the experiences a person had during childhood. When a child is raised with care, support, and in a loving environment, he/she develop a healthy sense of self. While a child who is raised without love and support in an environment, will experience neglect, rejection, loneliness, abuse and may end up with identity crises in future.

What Should I Do If I Do not Know Who I Am?

- ❖ Get to know yourself better through the eye of God (His word) before you were formed in your mother womb, God knew you (Jeremiah 1:5) including your interests, likes, and dislikes.
- ❖ Find out what is important to you, including your beliefs, values, and goals.
- ❖ Take time to mediate, reflect, and understand yourself, learn about

who you are without outside pressure and influence.

- ❖ Take a personality test, go for a retreat to know yourself better, learn new thing you may not enjoy everything, but each challenge is a learning experience.
- ❖ Learn how to trust God, on what He said concerning you, lean not on your understanding and ask questions from God and family.
- ❖ Build greater self-awareness by practicing meditation/mindfulness.

For the purpose of this book, the focus will be on your identity in Christ.

The person whom you are and what people think you are… are completely different.

Your identity is not in what you do, what you know, where you have been, your job, acquisition, or accomplishment but your identity is in who you are, and whom God says you are.

One thing everybody needs to know before anything is to know Who Am I? my values and what I believe in that truly make me who I am. Who am I is a more important question than what I do. Why? Because if you ever discover who you are, everything falls into place but if you never discover it or where you want to go, life becomes miserable, frustrating, and confusing. The greatest discovery is not out there but within you. The moment you can identify who you are, the story changes, and then you can identify where you want to go, who you want to know, and what to do, and you will realise your purpose on earth. All these outward things result in connecting with yourself inwardly, and the only way you can define yourself is in Christ Jesus because anything outside of Christ is a crisis.

As you can see from the theory of Psychologist Erik Erikson who defined different stages of human developmental growth, each stage ends with relational dynamics surrounding the individual. He removed God from every stage of his theory, but God included all in the creation of man and the work of salvation. Your search for significance and worth should begin and end with the word of God.

Everything is grounded on God's creation of people in His own image. God said, "Let us make humankind in our image, according to our likeness." (Gen. 1:26) So God created humankind in his image, in the image of God he created them; male and female he created them.

Christ death paid the penalty for sins, and His resurrection gives you a new life, new goals, and new Hope. He has given us complete security and challenging purpose. These are based not on our abilities, but on His grace and the power of his Spirit. Christ wants us to be zealous and ambitious but not about our success or status. (For God has not command us to be successful but commanded us to be fruitful and multiple Genesis 1:28) if you understand His forgiveness and acceptance, you will pursue the right things Christ and his cause and you will be free to enjoy his love.

"For it is Christ's love that fuels our passion and holds us tightly, because we are convinced that he has given his life for all of us. This means all died with him, so that those who live should no longer live self-absorbed lives but lives that are poured out for him—the one who died for us and now lives again. (2 Corinthians 5:14-15 TPT)

You may be hurting emotionally, relationally, and spiritually because you are unaware of the extent of your wounds, and if you don't take steps towards healing and health, this will lead to a bigger problem. And this is because of a lack of objectivity, as a result to this, you fail to see reality of pain, hurt and anger in your lives.

The cause of a lack of objectivity maybe you cannot see the reality of life, afraid of the truth, and or you think that the situation is normal, and you build resilience around it to cope with the situation. At one point in life, we all experience hurt, loneliness, anxiety, resentment, and anger.

As a believer and nonbeliever, we experience different emotions from time to time but the ability to control it makes the difference. Sometimes we build defence mechanisms to block pain and gain significance. We try to fill the void in our heart with material things or wearing a mask to cover up and pretending to be who you are not, and a sense of need would propel us to look for alternative. All we need to fill that void is Jesus Christ and the Holy Spirit to guide, direct, love and encourage us through others who is willing to help us.

Some of us have deep emotional and spiritual scars resulting from the neglect abuse and mind manipulation that often-accompanying living in a dysfunctional family with alcoholism, drug abuse, divorce, absent father, or mother, excessive anger, verbal and or physical abuse and so on, but all of us bear the effect of our own sinful nature and the imperfections of others. Whether your hurt is deep or relatively mild, it is wise to be honest about them in the context of a family relationship so that healing can begin.

Most of us mistakenly believe that God does not want us to be honest about our lives. We think that he will be upset with us if we tell him how we really feel. But the scripture tells us that God does not want us to be perfect or superficial in a relationship with him, with others or in our own lives. David wrote, "surely you desire truth in the inner parts you teach me wisdom in the innermost place "(Psalms 51:6) The Lord desires truth and honesty at the deepest level and want us also, to experience his love, forgiveness, and power in all areas of our lives. Experiencing his love does not mean that all our thoughts, emotions, and behaviours will be pleasant and pure. It means that we could be real, in our feelings, pain and joy, love and anger, frustration and confusion. The book of psalms gives us tremendous insight about what it's means to be honest with the Lord and others (Psalm 42:9) when you are in difficult despair situation like David read (Psalms 55:4-5, 13:1-2, for love to the lord read psalm (42:1-2).

When we have that void in our lives, when we are without something that we need, life becomes uncomfortable, miserable, frustrated, and even suicidal, because we have been conditioned to believed that it is necessary to perform to have any self-worth and be worthy of being loved. And as we come short of some specific standards, then we feel like a failure or unworthy of living a successful or a joyful life. The lie of having to work hard before you can successfully creep into our belief system and the truth is that God absolutely loved you completely, nothing you can do to stop it or increase His love for you. There is no need to go out of your way to perform for others who does not care about you or even to impress God because you are under His grace and that grace is sufficient for you. The options of others have no meaning to your self-worth, because of who you are in Christ Jesus, you are made in His image and likeness, and He is the only one that can determine your self-worth and significance/purpose in life.

For example, without water we become thirsty, without sleep we stay sleepy, life without value, purpose, or significance, we become miserable, and many people have killed themselves, because of this.

Jesus gave His life for our ramson for our lives, the price is unquantifiable that we cannot count it.

God told us that we are more valuable to Him than many sparrows, (Mathew 10:31) very significant to Him that He watches over us Day and Night, keep an eye on us, He cares so much about us that He numbered the hairs on our head, our welfare is very important to Him, He created all that we needed on earth before we arrived, while He skilfully knitted us in our mother's womb. For You formed my inward parts; You covered me in my mother's womb.

The God That Sees Knows All About You (Psalm 139:1-23)

I will praise You, for I am fearfully *and* wonderfully made; Marvellous are Your works, and *that* my soul knows very well.

My frame was not hidden from You When I was made in secret. *And* skilfully wrought in the lowest parts of the earth.

Your eyes saw my substance, being yet unformed. And in Your book, they all were written, the days fashioned for me,

When *as yet there were* none of them. How precious also are Your thoughts to me, O God! How great is the sum of them! *If* I should count them, they would be more in number than the sand; When I awake, I am still with You. (Psalm 139:13-18 NKJV).

In His love letter to us through the word, God told us to be careful of our choice, and because we are too precious to Him, and our lives are valuable. He kept reminding us in His word.

The bible has given us so much information for discovering our true significance and worth. In the book of Genesis 1 and 2, recounts man's creation, unveiling man's intended purpose (to honour Him) and man's value (Why man is a special creation). The plan of God for our lives is to have and live a life of abundance, through Christ (John 10:10) and how much He treasure us a His children. However, this believer needs to know that this life of abundance is lived in this wicked world filled with pain, rejection, abandonment, failure, grief, loneliness, sickness and even death, so this abundance life does not promise us trouble free. For in this unbelieving **world**, you **will** experience **trouble** and sorrows, **but** you must be courageous, for I have conquered the **world**!" **(John 16:33 TPT)**

"Therefore, as God's chosen people, holy and dearly loved, clothe yourselves with compassion, kindness, humility, gentleness, and patience. Bear with each other and forgive one another if any of you has a grievance against someone. Forgive as the Lord forgave you. And over all these virtues put on love, which binds them all together in perfect unity." Colossians 3:12-14, NIV

Chapter 4

Discovering Who You are

Who are you, who are you?

Research says that 80 % of children are always optimistic about themselves during their primary school years; but that belief drops to about 20% for those who maintain good self-esteem in secondary school or college. This number reduces to 5% for people that have positive image, while in the university and by the time of their graduation

With age, our confidence and the knowledge or acceptance of who we are decreases. Generally, when we were children, we all thought with enthusiasm, that we could climb the moon. By the time we get to college, we can hardly get out of bed. For all of us, this has been a common thread. In this publication, we will address the reader from the perspective of you, as the recipient of the news that God wants to give to us, to receive it and believe it – that means we are challenged to reflect and accept ourselves as that one individual who matters to God - You!

Discovering who you are therefore defines you, what you do, how you do it, claim your inheritance and your rights as a child of God. Your identity is the key to who you really are, and not what you do, what you have, or who you know, no matter the situation in life, never refer to yourself as merely a role that you play, but totally depend on what God says you are in His word.

Who are I, is more important question than what you do. If you ever discover who you are, everything falls into place but if you never discover it or where you want to go, you become miserable and frustrated. The greatest discovering is not out there but it is within you. When you identify who you are, then you will have clarity about where you want to go, who you want to know, what to do, as all these outward things result in connecting with yourself inwardly.

According to 1st Peter 2:9, You are a chosen generation; a royal priesthood, you are made for a purpose. How many of you have actually asked God to reveal to you, who you really are and your purpose?, As a chosen people we have to be careful, the people we associate ourselves with, they can make or break us, the Bible says if you walk with wise, you will be wise, but if you walk with fools, you will be foolish, Do not be deceived: "Evil company corrupts good habits." (I Corinthians 15:33, NKJV)

We are a Royal Priesthood, (Having a status of a King or a Queen, A member of a royal family. That is a double title royal, and priest of God born to be great. We are led by the ruler of the universe, which means you belong to the King of all Kings, Lord of all Lords, Ancient of days, the one that knows the end from the beginning.

We should learn to be like a lion, do you know that the lion is not the most powerful animal in the bush, but because he walks with authority and confidence, that makes all other animals to run from him, therefore, we should be like wise, so that the demons can recognise you and bow because He that is in you is greater than he that is in the world. This can only happen when you know who you are.

A Holy Nation, the word "holy" means "dedicated wholly to God's purposes without blemish or defect." The Old Testament Temple and its furnishings were never used for anything else but the worship of the Lord. These things used in God's service were to be carefully kept clean and pure always and never allowed to be polluted or contaminated. They were never used for anything else. Christians are meant to sacrifice themselves (body) to be "holy" which means dedicated only to the service of the Lord. (Romans 12:1) You are not to allow any corruption to enter you, and if it does, you are to confess it immediately to the Lord and let Him "cleanse you from all unrighteousness." Reading the word makes you holy, having been washed by the blood of Jesus.

As peculiar people, we are odd, unusual, and supernatural, do not compare yourself to the people of the world. You should endeavour to encourage each other, stop back biting, gossiping, and fighting. You do not trust each other anymore because we have no confidence in ourselves. We should be our brother's keeper.

You are Gods ambassador on earth, as well as ambassadors for Christ. As if God was pleading on your behalf, He said He implore you on Christ's behalf, be reconciled to God. (II Corinthians 5:20 NKJV) when you are an ambassador you a country's representative and every of your needs is taken care of by that country, not even a police officer of the resident country can arrest you, so we are supposed to be a representative of God here on earth,

And my God shall supply all your need according to His riches in glory by Christ Jesus. (Philippians 4:19 NKJV). But seek first the kingdom of God and His righteousness, and all these things shall be added to you. Therefore, do not worry about tomorrow, for tomorrow will worry about its own things. Sufficient for the day is its own trouble. (Matthew 6:33, 34 NKJV). The problem now is that people want other things before seeking God.

When you are asked who are you? Would you say I am a lawyer, a businessperson, doctor, mother, father, nurse, midwife, fashion designer, singer, footballer, farmer etc.

Reality is, that is not who you are but what you do.

Who are you, thus remains the key question - Who are you?

When it comes to knowing who you are, there are things you need to know about your inheritance and rights. It is good to know your heritage.

Heritage is where you come from, it moulds one and sharpens your paradigm, what you do, your associates, the books you read and your vision in life is tied to your heritage.

In order to know who you are, you must know where you came from, e. g English Caucasian, African, Caribbean, American, India or Asia background, and the most important one is heavenly heritage, as we belong to the family of God. The bible says that, before you were born God knew you and ordained you to be a prophet unto nations. I discover that I am not a part of the lower class, middle class, working class nor upper class. I belong to God's class - and based on the above knowledge, and that is where you belong as well.

Your heritage sharpens you. You do not only have your biological heritage, but your spiritual heritage too. Psalm 16:6 says: *O Lord, you are the portion of my inheritance and my cup; You maintain my lot. The lines have fallen to me in pleasant places; Yes, I have a good inheritance.*

"All praise to God, the Father of our Lord Jesus Christ, who has blessed us with every spiritual blessing in the heavenly realms because we are united with Christ. Even before he made the world, God loved us and chose us in Christ to be holy and without fault in his eyes. God decided in advance to adopt us into his own family by bringing us to himself through Jesus Christ. This is what he wanted to do, and it gave him great pleasure." (Ephesians 1:3-5)

Some nuggets that will help you define You Identify:

Knowing who you are, speaks of your identity,

knowing where you come from, speaks of your heritage,

knowing what you were born into, speaks of Inheritance, born again into the kingdom of God.

knowing why you were born, speaks of your purpose.

knowing where you are going to in life, speaks of destiny.

knowing what you will do when you get there, speaks of your assignments,

knowing why you are doing what you are doing when you get there, speaks of your mission and vision.

Knowing whom (people) you are going to go with, speaks of your relationship.

Knowing how to plan the things you going to do and underwrite, speaks of your resources.

Knowing when to do it, speaks of your time and season.

Knowing how people will know that you did, it when you die, speaks of your legacy.

Knowing all these 11 things of who you are, will set you apart, and distinguished you from others.

If you do not know who you are, others will tell you who you are not, and the devil will rob you of your joy and kick you like a ball.

Who are you, who are you?

This question was once asked of a powerful man of God, John the Baptist, Who Are You? And he replied, I am a voice crying out in the wilderness.

"Now this is the testimony of John, when the Jews sent priests and Levites from Jerusalem to ask him, "Who are you?" He confessed, and did not deny, but confessed, "I am not the Christ." And they asked him, "What then? Are you Elijah?" He said, "I am not." "Are you the Prophet?" And he answered, "No." Then they said to him, "Who are you, that we may give an answer to those who sent us? What do you say about yourself?" He said: "I am 'The voice of one crying in the wilderness: "Make straight the way of the LORD," as the prophet Isaiah said."" John 1:19-23, NKJV

I dare to ask you that same question today, *who are you*?

The answer, most people would have given will be, I am John the son of Zechariah, my mother is Elizabeth, the sister to Mary the mother of Jesus. I am a prophet of God; I eat wild honey and live in the wilderness. But when he was asked who are you? He said I am not Christ; John was teaching us about our identity, our foundation, the Rock of our identity is this, Christ our solid rock/foundation.

There is a God, and you are not Him, John the Baptist said I am not the Messiah, before you know who you are, you must first know who you are not,

John said before I identity who I am, I will tell you who I am not, but

that I am the creation not the creator, I am the sheep, not the shepherd, I am the clay not the porter, I am the son, not the father, I am the servant not the master, I am not God but a child of God.

Some of us will be free from the moment you know the revelation that there is a God, and you are not Him, by trusting God with your whole heart and not leaning on your own understanding. (Proverbs 3:6-6)

Only then you will stop crying when people do not sing song of praise to you, bowing to you, or sharing of God's glory.

He said again, I am not Elijah, not Moses, I may talk like them, walk, or eat like them, even wear clothes like them, but I am not the same, I am different, unique and I do not want to be someone else. It is essential to know who you are not, before you can know who you are, it is particularly important to know what you are called to do, not somebody whom God has not called you to be, or else you will be frustrated, and not be happy. Most people seek to fit in; when God had not anointed us to stand in those positions.

John the Baptist said I am who God, said I am, I have been ordained before; I was formed in my mother's womb. It is said in the bible that the prophet Isaiah foretold (prophesied) long before I was born, thus; you are who God said you are - a royal priesthood, chosen generation. John did not say I am John, or a son of Elizabeth, a preacher, pastor, an evangelist, bishop - rather he said that I am who

God says I am.

You could be or not be successful, as long as you believe, you are still Who God says you are.

No matter what - *I am who God says I am*; I may have failed many times, but it does not change who I am; or I may have missed my way, yet I am who God calls me. You must understand today who you are in Christ Jesus.

In creation, God called every other thing into existence. When He came to you, He touched and moulded you, and He breathe life into you. He says you were good, He formed and fashioned you with His hands. This is reason why some people are looking for someone to *touch* them, even when they have been abused, it is due to a void that is inside of them, this can only be found in Christ. Something might feel, taste, or look like God's touch or impact, yet it is not. We hear of the Woman with the issue of blood in the bible. She was healed after touching Jesus's garment – His power touched her. In other words, until He touches that issue of blood in your life, it will not change or stop immediately.

When He touches one, it brings them healing, deliverance, freedom, joy, peace, and love.

When He touches one, a life in crisis becomes calm, does not get crushed, but is restored.

When God created you, He brought you as Himself into existence; made you in His image. Animals do not have what you have, nor the trees. Only humanity like you and I have the special touch.

When John said I am not Elijah, what did that say of him? It meant "*I do not want to fit in,*" as it may sacrifice his identity. We must be willing to change our weaknesses and turn them into strengths when possible. If this is not possible, we seek opportunities in which God can be glorified - even in our failures and suffering. Someone with a positive sense of self-esteem enjoys personal strengths and are aware of weaknesses – which is wholesome love for oneself.

God does not make mistakes, and He is never finished working in us as He continues to refine and edify you, helping each of us to reach our maximum potentials 1 peter,5:10) negatives can be changed into positive and tragedies into triumphs with the saviour's touch.

We see that it is unsurprising as our enemy, the devil hates humankind as the bible states – as His creation, you remind him of God who is also his creator - of the enemies as well. You and I are made in God's image and the enemy knows this – which threatens him, so he fights God's people – those who love Him. One verse in Psalms chapter 20 says '*Some trust in horses, some in chariot but you will remember to trust in the lord God'*. God did not only make you in his image, but He also blessed you.

God however, cursed Satan when he caused the man to fall. He cursed a woman's *childbearing* with pain and a man with sweat for his labour as they violated God's instruction. But never cursed the man and the woman per se, though they failed God and fell. God blessed us, you and I. God sees you He says you are good; it does not matter what others say or think about you, God said He loves you. Thus, you should 'n*ever*' be confused about your position with your *condition* or *circumstances* in life.

A baby without a parent will live, one day that child will grow but he will remain the child of their parents. Do not ever judge a tree by the season, because the tree will still change. See, your season may change but your identity will *never* change.

John said if you know who you are, you will no longer echo what others are saying, and you become a voice to your generation that speaks to God and about God. When you know who you are, you can talk about God not your problems or negative issues in your life. You do not talk about your mountain; rather talk to your mountain to move into the sea, by the authority given to you (Luke 10:19)

The bible admonishes us not to conform to the world; but to transform our minds.

"And do not be conformed to this world, but be transformed by the renewing of your mind, that you may prove what is that good and acceptable and perfect will of God."

Romans 12:2 NKJV

Are You Conforming To The World, To Your Peers, Or Your Environment?

Let me tell you a story that I read in a book written by Proctor Gallagher (Are you a Pink Elephant?) that changed my life, and it might resonate with you as well.

"Once upon a time a pink elephant was born. He was so clearly different from the rest that soon the grey elephants started to distance themselves and ignore him.

The little pink elephant felt incredibly sad, rejected, and abandoned by family and friends.

He realised that to fit in with the rest of the herd, he had to be like one of them.

So, he covered himself with mud and dirt until he became like a dirty grey elephant. Throughout the years he kept covering himself and hiding behind the dirt. Then one day, rain began pouring down and washed away all the mud and dirt from his body. He was pink again! Woohoo.. shouted the rest of the elephants with surprise! The grey elephants turned and started laughing at the sight of his obvious pinkness.

As the laughter grew louder, he realised that he was trying to fit into a group that would never understand him nor accept him for who he is. He knew that he was different and that he needed to find a group of pink elephants just like him, where he would be accepted and learn to love himself as he was. Then the journey of self-discovery and self-love began that day.

Now Imagine yourself as an "Elephant," the largest land animal on earth. An elephant is too massive to miss. It has an enormous amount of power. If you were a *Pink Elephant* when you were born, then you would be different from most people around you. People will think that you are a bit strange when they meet you and because of this, you may wish to hide your true self and ***True Identity.***

You make every effort to fit in, yet people always notice you. Sometimes you will be admired for being different. Unfortunately, we are often ridiculed. Then the opportunity is, you have one of two choices to make. You gather your strength and remain proud that you are Pink or attempt to convince everyone that you are exactly like them. Most people choose the second option. It seems easier to just fit in.

The truth is that it does not matter that people will laugh at, mock you, or

think that you are weird, or feel your dreams seem unattainable, whatever the excuses, you must not listen to them, because you are meant to be different.

These people are too fixed in their limited herd mentality to see the greater possibilities that are available. As a fellow ambassador of Christ teaching, encouraging hidden pink elephants to come out of their hiding shelf and become themselves, and that you are unique the way you are. Those that know their God shall be strong and do great exploit, just as you, from now, begin to do great and mighty things to the glory of the Father.

If you are willing to be anything to fit it, 10 years down the line, you would have forgotten who you are meant to be, do not conform to the world but be transformed, by the renewing of your mind (Romans 12:2)

Know who you are and therefore, do not be someone else.

You are not alone in that condition you found yourself, you can be yourself in the presence of others, remember all the successful people, the inventors and innovators were pink elephants who were not ashamed of who they are. *"An Idea Is Nothing Until You Put into Use"*

You must believe in yourself: You cannot act until you believe in your ability and in yourself to manage the consequences of your decisions and become accountable for your actions. Also embrace risk and make it your best friend as you give birth to your idea, then keep focus no matter the disruption on your way.

It takes a unique person to get to the moon, be a sporty person, a music icon or create personal computers. The herd (the chicken, group) is always afraid of innovative ideas, but unashamed.

'*Pink Elephants*' are never stopped! They are risk takers, hold cutting-edge belief in a field of expertise. Pink Elephants live in a world of possibilities, not fearful but boldness.

Bernard Hiller states that, "*What is different about you is what makes you special.*"

God's word says that *God has not given you the spirit of fear, but of power, love, and a sound mind.* (2 Timothy 1; 7)

Fear can be disabling and stop us in our tracks:

- Fear of failure (keeps you from trying)
- Fear of success (sabotages your every effort)
- Fear of looking foolish (keeps you from speaking up)
- Fear of speaking (keeps others from seeing your brilliance)
- Fear of loneliness (pushes you into unhealthy relationships)
- Fear of poverty (clouds your financial decisions or creates workaholics)

What Makes You Special?

"Your unique gifts and skills, the pieces of your personality, your life experiences, knowledge, and emotions. These qualities that make you unique can be honed, improved upon, and made to grow as you grow and learn along your life journey."

YOU are NOT condemned to a particular outcome.

"You are unique, and only **YOU** can do what you were sent here to do. (Article from *While everybody is trying to be like someone else, be different, be YOU! — Michael Mints*)"

""You are the light of the world. A city that is set on a hill cannot be hidden. Nor do they light a lamp and put it under a basket, but on a lampstand, and it gives light to all who are in the house. Let your light so shine before men, that they may see your good works and glorify your Father in heaven." Matthew 5:14-18NKJV

"If you can't fly then run, if you can't run then walk, if you can't walk then crawl, but whatever you do you have to keep moving forward." — Martin Luther King Jr.

No matter where you are and what your situation is, your focus can be shifted to something positive by spending a few minutes a day focusing on you. There are life lessons in all we experience, in every opportunity missed and taken, in every single person we encounter in our lives—they all offer us something unique and what we choose to do with those gifts is up to us. Writing them down is the simplest, most effective thing you can do every day to be happier.

"Positive thoughts have a power to change your life, when they are fuelled by positive emotions." Peggy McColl

Facts of Life to Consider

You Will Never Rise Above The Revelation Of Who You Are

You Will Never Rise Above Your Self Esteem, Worth, Respect,

You Will Never Rise Above Who You Think You Are,

And That Becomes A Leach That Will Hold You Back

You Can Do More, You Can Be Wild, Innovative, Creative

You Are Full Of Gifts, Talents, And Potential

But As Long As The Leach Is On You, You Will Live A Frustrated Life.

When You Start Feeling Sorry For Yourself, Holding Self-Pity Party

When You Start Saying My God Is Not Powerful, By What You Say

I Can Not Do This, It Is Not For Me, Oh It Is Too Hard, I Can Not, I Cannot

With Every Excuse In The Book, This Is But A Leach,

There Is No Way You Will Achieve Your Purpose, As Long As You Have The Leach On You.

The Dogs You See In The Park With The Leach On, No Matter How Wild, Or Terrifying The Dog May Like,

You Are Not Too Scared Of It, Why? Because The Leach Can Only Allow It To An Extent.

It Will Not Go As Far As It Want But To The Extend As The Chain Or Leach Allows It To

The Leach Places A Limit On You, Not God.

Your Lack Of Faith Places A Limit On You But God Created You Limitless

Not Knowing Who You Are, Places A Limit On Your Full Potential, Because You Are Still Acting Out Of Your Weaknesses, Out Of Your Background, Culture, And Environment Instead Of Acting On What God Says You Are, And Who God Is Inside Of You

Jesus said to the people He healed all the time, let it be to you according to your faith, He never said according to my power, or His glory, He said according to your faith.

Your faith, with who God is and who you are in Him is the leach that determines how far you can go in life. You do not see things the way they are, but you see things the way you are, that is why two different people see a glass of water half full while the other sees it empty, it is about your perception. When your perception changes, your world will change drastically. "The major key to your better future is you " (Jim Rohn.) and you become what you behold" (William Blake)

"It's wild that when you decide you are worth more, the Universe starts opening doors to make it a reality." Cory Allen, Podcaster-Mediation Teacher Audio Engineer

Before you begin a thing, remind yourself that difficulties and delays is quite impossible to foresee ahead. You can only see one thing clearly, and that is your goal. Form a mental vision of that and cling to it through thick and thin.

Kathleen Norris – Writer

Chapter 5

In Search of Significance:

Discovering Meaning and Purpose in Life

Introduction

"*Significance* is the quality of being worthy of attention or something necessary for a particular situation and of much importance. The fact that you are significant means, you are worthy, valued, esteemed, particularly important personality, phenomenally unique, and we were all created in God's image.

In Search of Significance explores an ever-existent universal human quest by which individuals can discover true meaning and purpose to this life and purpose to own existence.

In a world filled with troubles, challenges, distractions, responsibilities, and meaningless tasks; people find themselves yearning for something more. They thirst for significance, by looking for meaning and purpose which is in fact missing in life.

It is funny to know that we may always long to be for what, we already are. Our greatest need in life however is to become/ accept who we already are in Christ." Selah!

This was the reason that the devil was able to deceive Eve, in the Garden of Eden.

"The serpent replied, "You will not surely die. For, God knows that when you eat of it, your eyes will be opened, and you will be like God, knowing good and evil." Since the woman sought wisdom, she ate the fruit of the tree and gave some to Adam to eat too. (Genesis 3:4-5)

In this story, Eve had forgotten that she was a god over the Serpent and was looking for significance outside of God by allowing herself to be deceived and Adam to be disobedient.

I say: '*You are gods; you are all children of the Most-High God*' (Psalm 82:6), Selah!!

If you do not know who you are or where you are from, the devil will take advantage of you, your joy, peace, finance, marriage, career, business, job, and destiny.

Jesus said in (John 8:32 TPT) that if you embrace the truth, it will release true freedom into your life." He was not only referring to the intellectual consent to truth but also to how you apply the truth (word of God) to any situation or issue, your motives, identity, and self-worth.

Exploring Personal Values and Beliefs

One way to embark on a journey in search of significance is by examining our values and beliefs. By understanding who you really are and what truly matters to you, you can align your actions with your deepest convictions. This intentional effort allows us to live our lives in a purpose-driven manner and find fulfilment in our pursuits.

Moreover, most people do not fully know who they are in Christ and as such allow insignificant things or challenges to affect their self-worth and self-esteem radically. In addition, they continue to look for security and purpose outside of God like worldly things, personal success, status, fame, money, outward appearance, and approval from other people. All these may give you temporary happiness and there will be no joy in you but a void that can only be filled by God. And the more you seek for these worldly resources the bigger the void in you.

You need to get off this worldly race and hopelessness and get back to the basic truth that can help you to live for Christ Jesus instead of looking for people's approval and validation in material things. Jesus died to make you whole, and He has paid the full price for your freedom, new life, new hope, and peace of mind. You are complete in Him who is the head of all principality and power and has also given you security and purpose.

You have been ordained by God right from your mother's womb, set apart for His glory, and holy in His eyes without fault. God decided this in advance and has adopted you into his own family by bringing you to himself through Jesus Christ. This is what he wanted to do, and it gave Him great pleasure. Whatever you are today, is not based on your ability but on the grace of God and the power of the Holy Spirit.

Pursuing Passion and Purpose:

Discovering our passions and pursuing them can ignite a sense of significance in our lives. When we engage in activities that bring us joy and tap into our unique talents and strengths, our approach to life changes. We feel a deep sense of fulfilment, as our actions align with our authentic selves.

God's plan for your life is good, not evil, and to bring you to an expected end. So, any other plan outside of God's plan for you, causes you to be yearning for significance in worldly things. You need patience and perseverance, knowing that God's promises over your life to rescue you from challenges, suffering, and pains may be delayed, and not denied, but rather **a** promise that God has a plan for your life and regardless of your current situation, He can do exceedingly, abundantly above all that you ask or think, to prosper and give you hope and future. For I know the plans *and* thoughts that I have for you,' says the Lord, 'plans for peace *and* well-being and not for disaster, to give you a future and a hope. (Jeremiah 29:11)

This is the truth that will enable you to get out of bed each morning and face the delight and despair of this world. This truth will enable you to cope with success and failure without missing a step, will set you up to walk humbly and confidently with Christ through the day and enable you to reflect on the day that has passed with repentance and faith and to go to sleep resting in the peace that flows from God's forgiveness. Knowing yourself through the scripture is the best peaceful practical, and most important truth there is to sustain you in our falling and wicked world.

Knowing who you are in Christ, lays the foundation for your identity and helps to build a pathway to security, significance, and satisfaction in life.

Your self-worth is not based on your performance, achievement, environment, or family that you came through into the world or the opinions of others.

"Your significance or self-worth is based on what Jesus Christ had done for you on the cross, not what you have done or your performance". Carol Babalola

The Bible says "For we all have become like one who is [ceremonially] unclean [like a leper], And all our deeds of righteousness are like filthy rags; We all wither and decay like a leaf, and our wickedness [our sin, our injustice, our wrongdoing], like the wind, takes us away [carrying us far from God's favour, toward destruction]. (Isaiah 64:6) Because of Jesus Christ and His redemption, you are completely forgiven of your sins, and fully pleasing to God, and you are totally accepted by God as His precious child.

There is a void in everyone's heart who is without Jesus in their life. Everyone is searching for significance, the original you, your search should begin with God and end with God because He is your manufacturer, who intricately formed you in the womb. In addition, you must never copy or repeat what others have done, or doing, you are uniquely different, an express image of God and your DNA has specific traits, personalities and potentials that no one else can ever fulfil.

Rather than seeking security and purpose from worldly resources such as materialism, fame, beauty, wealth, achievements, and people's approval, which last but for a while.

"If you do not know who you are, your search and accumulation, of achievements and self-actualisation will end in despair" Carol Babalola

This brings me to Maslow's theory that says self-actualisation, in psychology, is "a concept regarding the process by which an individual reaches his or her full potential. It was originally introduced by Kurt Goldstein, a physician specialising in neuroanatomy and psychiatry in the early half of the 20th century". or

"self-actualisation is when a person can do what they feel they are "meant" to do and be who they are "meant" to be. The need for self-actualisation is present in all of us but can only be met once all the lower needs are sufficiently satisfied, according to Psychology.

But the word of God tells you that His will for your life as a believer is opposite to the theory of Psychology.

This theory is not true but a fact. And the truth is to seek first the kingdom of God and His righteousness, and all these things shall be added unto you. (Mathew 6:33)

Connection and Contribution

Significance or meaningfulness often arises from our relationships with God. God-created relationships, when He said, "Let us make man in our image and our likeness, and He created them male and female "in his own image," he blesses them and charges them to rule over the rest of creation, and interactions with others". Investing in meaningful connections, fostering empathy, and embracing opportunities to contribute positively to the lives of those around you can all lead to a greater sense of significance. Through acts of kindness, volunteering, or mentoring, we can find purpose in making a difference in the lives of others.

The death of Jesus Christ on the cross paid for the penalty of your sins, He declared you not guilty, and sanctified for His glory. And His resurrection gave you a new life, hope, peace, joy, patience, kindness, gentleness, and self-control. He has given you complete security and challenging purposes that are not based on your talents, gifts, abilities, power, and or your might. And they are based on the grace of God and the power of His Spirit. Christ indeed wants you to be intense and ambitious in pursuit of the plan of God for your life, but not about your success, material things, or self-actualisation. As you understand God's forgiveness and acceptance of you, you will be intense about evangelism, winning souls for His kingdom, which is the heartbeat of God, loving God, loving your neighbours, Christ, and His cause, and then you will be free to enjoy the benefits that come with salvation.

You may have suffered from the devastating effects of shame, so overpowering, or so disappointing to us that it creates a permanently negative opinion about your self-worth. Others may not know of our features, but we do. We may only imagine their rejection, but being real or imaging the pain resulting from it cripples our confidence and hope.

Shame usually results in guilt and self-depreciation, but it can also lead us to search for God and His answers. Our inner, undeniable need for personal significance can created to make our search for Him. He alone can fulfil our deep needs. In Him, we find peace, acceptance, and love, through Him, we find the courage and power to develop into the men and women He intends us to be. Although Satan wants to convince us that we will always be prisoners of our failures and past experiences, by God's grace we can be freed from the guilt of our past and experience a renewed purpose for our lives.

Shame is the emotional tar of your life, and you can only get rid of it with the help of God. Shame and rejection can impact people's self-esteem adversely, and these can manifest itself in different ways.

Inferiority: The feelings of inferiority come from prolonged patterns of failures or past experiences of hurts, all these can affect your self-worth, emotions, and behaviour.

Reflecting on Life's Challenges and Transitions:

Challenging moments and significant life transitions often force us to question our values, beliefs, and purpose in life. By embracing these moments of uncertainty, we can gain valuable insights about ourselves and our desires. As we reflect and grow from these experiences, we widen our search for significance, deepening our understanding of what truly matters.

Conclusion

The central question man must face in life are who am I? And why am I here? These questions relate directly to a man's search for self-worth, and significance. The world has programmed us with a specific system of evaluating ourselves. This system is contrary to God system, no matter what our standard of performance is or whose approval we are seeking. The world system will allow us fleeting moments of success and pride, but it will never let us enjoy lasting personal significance. Success and approval cannot ultimately fulfil our need for self-worth or significance.

Chapter 6

Understanding What Defines Our worth

As believers our fulfilment in this life does not depend on our skills to avoid problems in life but on the ability to apply the word of God appropriately as a specific solution to these problems. A ***sound understanding of God's truth*** is the first step toward discovering our significance and worth.

Due to inadequate and false teaching in some churches and seeking of solution from secular sources concerning our identity and self-worth. As a result of this distort self-perception, some people are experiencing hopelessness instead of a rich and meaningful life that God intended for us. Moreover, Satan continue to deceive us, into believing that the basis of our worth is in our performance and our ability to please other, and that you are not good enough for the job, you are not beautiful, not qualify for the job, you are love by God, you are alone and not accepted into the family of God and that because you have failed in a project , that makes you a failure, No!

Your significance and self-worth are based on what God said about you (the word of God, truth) through faith. Nothing more, nothing less. Let's visit the equation we have spoken about in other areas in this book.

The Equation that reflects the lies of the devil:

Self-worth = performance = Peoples' Opinions

The Equation that reflects the truth of God:

Self-worth = what God's Truth says about You.

Understanding our worth is linked to finding our true significance in life.

It is in the discovery and knowing who you are in Christ Jesus, and it is an ongoing journey that is unique to everyone. It is a continuous pursuit that requires self-reflection, exploration, and a willingness to embrace the word of God and the Holy Spirit. By delving into the word, and your values, pursuing your passions, cultivating, a connection with God and others, embracing life's challenges, and practicing meditation on the word and journalling, you can unearth deeper meaning and purpose in your lives. In this quest, you may discover that significance is not a single destination but a lifelong journey of growth in every area of your life, fulfilment, and seeking the kingdom of God and His righteousness, and all these things shall be added to you.

Maslow's Hierarchy of Needs versus God's Hierarchy of Needs

The **definition of self-actualisation**, in Maslow's theory, is different from how **God wants His children to fulfil or actualise His purpose for their life.**

The concept of self-actualisation comes from Maslow's theory of human motivation. He said that unsatisfied needs drive people's behaviour and that when those needs like food, water, and safety are met, they become more motivated to meet other needs such as social connection and self-esteem when all these are met, then they will move to pursue self-actualisation. "*According to Maslow self-actualisation is about achieving full potential, which is morality, creativity, and problem-solving.*"

In Maslow's last book, before his death, he suggested that the highest form of self-actualisation transcends the self. We then strive to be selfless and contribute to something purposeful that is greater than ourselves (Greene, & Burke, 2007).

This is also referred to as "*Beyond Self-Actualisation*" *or* "*Transcendence*".

You see this beyond actualisation or transcendence refers to God, the creator of heaven and the earth. In everything that God made on earth, there is always a counterfeit fake made by the devil, who always wants to compete with God. In Maslow's hierarchy of needs, he stated that as humans, you needed the basic things of life to attain self-actualisation, and God said "But seek first His Kingdom and His righteousness, and all these things will be given to you as well. Therefore, do not worry about tomorrow, for tomorrow will worry about itself. Each day has enough trouble of its own." (Matt. 6:33,34). Jesus encourages and commands us not to worry about 'things' such as provision, money, clothes, houses, possessions, and what will happen tomorrow. He told us not to be obsessed with things or be stressed out about things.

Basic Physical Needs

This first level of need includes the basic requirements for survival, such as food, water, shelter, and sleep. From God's perspective, by

"His divine power *has* granted to us *all things* that *pertain* to *life* and *godliness*, through the knowledge of him who called us to his own glory and excellence. (2peter 1:3") because of His divine providence, He said, *do not worry (anxious) about what you will eat, drink, shelter, or wear* (Mathew 5:25).

Jesus was saying that worry is unproductive. Worry keeps you from fulfilling the kingdom purposes to which He has called you. God uses all situations to accomplish His purposes, and He wants you to trust and rely absolutely, on Him in every area of your life. Remember that 'things' are only temporary possessions. You did not bring anything into this world, and you certainly cannot take anything with you when you die. You will leave everything behind, so maintain the right perspective when the temptation comes to worry about 'things. Live with God as your Source and Helper in all areas of your life.

Safety and Security:

This second level includes feelings of safety and security, both externally and internally. It involves protection from physical harm, emotional stability, and a sense of belonging. God's vision is for you to accept Jesus as your saviour, and you shall be saved, redeemed, forgiven, accepted, and protected from all evil, and you are to dwell and abide under the shadow of the Almighty for your security both externally and internally.

Love and Belonging:

This third level includes the need for intimate relationships, social connections, and a sense of belonging within a community. From a spiritual perspective, God loves and cherishes relationships, which was why He would visit Adam and Eve at the cool of the day(Genesis 3:8) Also, He instituted marriages because of relationships, and finally, he admonished that you should not forsake the gathering of your brethren, He wants you to belong to your community, connecting, who share the same beliefs and experiencing love and compassion. Destiny fulfilment is impossible without relationships, associations, and connections. (Apostle Joshua Selman) your relationship with Jesus, made it possible for you to be reconcile back to God, relationship are advantageous connections, which are mutually beneficial to the parties involved. The easiest way to (succeed) make it in life are through relationships and connections, (Gen 13:1) What God gave Abraham, He also gave Lot.

Esteem and Self-Worth:

This fourth level encompasses self-esteem, self-confidence, and a sense of personal value and worth. From God's standpoint, you were made in His image and the Holy Spirit dwells inside of you. Knowing that you were made in God's image increases your self-worth and self-esteem, and the word of God gives you confidence and high esteem, in the sight of God and man (Proverbs 3:4) and living in alignment with one's spiritual values.

Self-Actualization:

This fifth level refers to fulfilling one's potential, pursuing personal growth, and striving for self-fulfilment. From God's viewpoint, you are to be in alignment with God's purpose for your life, beliefs, and values and seek a deeper connection with God. "But seek first His Kingdom and His righteousness, and all these things will be given to you as well. Therefore, do not worry about tomorrow, for tomorrow will worry about itself. Each day has enough trouble of its own." (Matt. 6:33,34).

Transcendence and Meaning:

This sixth and final level involves reaching beyond oneself and seeking God the author and finisher of your faith, (transcendence). It comes with the desire for connection to something greater than yourself, finding meaning and purpose in life, and experiencing a sense of awe, wonder, and spiritual fulfilment. It encompasses connection with God, the creator of heaven and the earth, and living according to the teachings of Jesus and the word of God.

When God created man, He gave him a sense of purpose. After man disobeyed God, he lost his sense of the significance of God. Since then, man has tried to find purpose and meaning away from God. However, God made us in a way that He is the only one who can meet our spiritual and physical needs money, fame, material things, achievements, success, and prestige in each profession are, only fake, of the true significance we have in Christ because you are complete in Him. Moreover, these counterfeits promise are to meet our need for fulfilment, and what they provide is always short-lived. God and His purpose alone can give you a lasting sense of significance.

Maslow's Hierarchy of Need – graphic context:

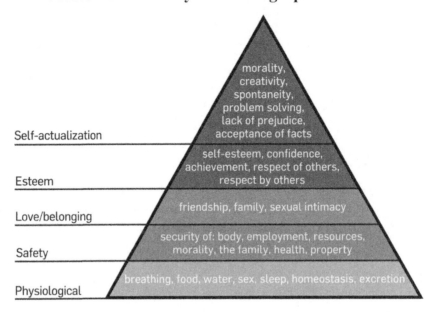

God's Hierarchy of Needs

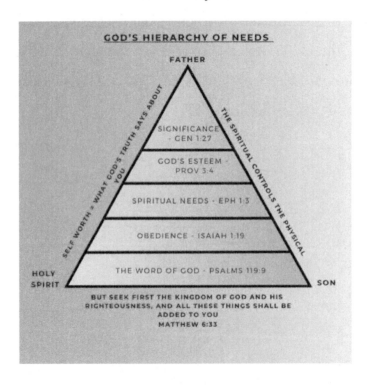

Chapter 7

Your Identity - Chosen by God.

And in love, God chose you and I before he laid the foundation of the universe!

Because of his great love, he ordained us, so that we would be seen as holy in his eyes with an unstained innocence. (Ephesians, 1:4TPT)

In knowing your identity, the first step is to ensure that you know who you are as a child of God, as those who are chosen by God before the foundation of the earth, and that you have been united to the Lord Jesus Christ. The God of the universe handpicked you and set you apart for His purpose. God chose you out of the millions of sperms that swam across into your mother's **Womb** because He wanted you to be His, to fellowship with you as He did with Adam and Eve in the garden of Eden (Genesis 3:8).

God chose you as a friend, partner, to walk with you and to display you in this world as a pearl of great price. He chose you because He loved you before the foundation of the earth, (Ephesians 1:4) and before any star in the sky, any tree or stream of water flowing.

Your name is written in the palm of His hands, carried you in His heart, and gave you a destiny before the creation of anything on earth. The helper of the hopeless chose you to experience *the wealth of God's glorious inheritances that he finds in you and t*o show you the hope of His calling (Ephesians 1:18-21); and the hope that you will, one day be like Christ through transformation by the renewing of your mind (Romans 12:2).

You were born to lead, built to help others move forward and chosen to rise as a solution provider for such a time as this.

Daily Devotional

&

Journaling

Daily Devotional And Journaling

You are welcome to this transformational daily devotional journal, which is aimed to help you understand who you are as a Son of God, a seed of righteousness, a saint, a warrior, and a servant of the Mos- High God.

I Pray and hope that this session will encourage, strengthen, and uplift your faith. That the discovery of your identity in Christ Jesus, will help you get more clarity, reassurance and peace of God that passes all understanding. As part of this, knowing your identity in Christ and readiness to accept who we are, I encourage readers to engage in Daily Devotional and Journaling; ahead. Thank you and remain blessed.

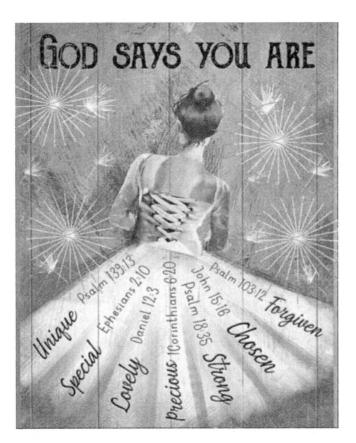

DAY 1: You Are Chosen by God

Do you know that you were chosen by God Himself before the foundation of the earth?

Do you know that you have been united to the Lord Jesus Christ?

How would your life be different, now that you know you are specifically chosen by God, as an individual?

....
....
....
....
....
....
....
....
....
....
....
....

DAY 2: Ponder on Uniquely Chosen

How does it make you feel that you are uniquely chosen? (Selah)

Do know how special you are because you are chosen?

....
....
....

....
....
....
....
....
....
....
....
....

DAY 3: The Apple of God's Eye

You are the apple of His eyes; do you feel like you are the apple of His?

Now write down your thoughts and feelings and your daily application:

....
....
....
....
....
....
....
....
....
....
....

Prayer

Lord, I praise and thank you for choosing you, for making me the apple of your eyes, and the treasure of your heart. Thank you, Lord, that I am special, Lord help, me understand how much you love me and give me the courage to fully embrace God given identity.

Day 4: Prayer Requests

....

....

....

....

....

....

....

....

....

....

Day 5: Meditation of Scriptures

....

....

....

....

....

....
....
....
....
....
....
....
....

Day 6: Reflection

....
....
....
....
....
....
....
....
....
....
....
....
....
....

Day 7: Application

Now write down your thoughts, prayers answered, gratitude and your daily application.

What changes do you need to make in your life to accept God's love?

....
....
....
....
....
....
....
....
....
....
....
....

Day 8: Prayers Answered

....
....
....
....
....
....
....
....

....

....

....

....

....

Day 9: Gratitude.

Why are you thankful? Name 5 Things for Which You are Grateful.

....

....

....

....

....

....

....

....

....

....

....

....

....

....

....

Deeper Learning: Adopted by God.

For it was always in his perfect plan to adopt us as his delightful children, through our union with Jesus, the Anointed One, so that his tremendous love that cascades over us would glorify his grace —for the same love he has for the Beloved, Jesus, he has for us. (Ephesians, 1:5, TPT)

In the process of adoption, an individual whether relative or not assumes parental responsibilities for the child of another, as Mordecai adopted his young relative Esther after the death of her parents. Joseph adopted Jesus to be recognised as his own son in the eyes of God and man.

This gave all legal inheritance rights traceable through Joseph to Jesus (Matthew 1:1-25) assigning to him a legal claim to the Davidic throne. And spiritually we are the children of God by adoption just as Jesus was the child of Joseph by adoption.

This process of adoption gives the one adopted full family standing and rights (Romance 8: 15-18). This transaction is divinely authorised, God blessed and legally binding means for adding to the family unit and passing on the family inheritance (Galatians 4:5, Ephesians 1:5)

When you accept Jesus as your saviour and Lord, the Holy Spirit completes a transaction of adoption on your behalf. You become God's child, and He is your ABBA Father. As God's adopted child you will inherit a perfect home with him, (Romans 8:15, Galatians 4:6) and for the moment, you have immediate access to Him for comfort, direction, and provision. He adopted you with pleasure and will never revoke your adoption. (Selah)

You are adopted by God into His family through your union with Jesus Christ. At the set time, God sent His begotten son, born of a woman under the law, to die for you so that you may receive your freedom from the slavering of the law. Everyone had sinned right from the first Adam and had come short of the glory of God and needed to be redeemed and rescued from bondage to enter the new family of God through the death and resurrection of Jesus Christ. (Selah)

Since you have been adopted into the family of God by His grace, you now have access to Him in an intimate kind of fellowship (Matthew 6:32).

Adoption means both redemption and the new relation of trust and love, for "because you are sons, God has sent forth the Spirit of His Son into your hearts, crying, Abba, Father" (vs 6). The adoption freed us from slavery to sonship and inheritance, you are irreplaceable, a begotten child of God's family, His beloved child of inestimable value and you belong to royal family as your Father is the King of all kings.

DAY 10 – Adopted by God

What do you think about adoption? How do you feel, being adopted into God's family?

....

....

....

....

....

....

....

....

....

....

....

....

DAY 11 : Intimacy with God

How do you get access to God in an intimate fellowship? Can you explain how the Holy Spirit completes a transaction of adoption on your behalf? (Selah)

....

....

....

....

....

....

....

....

....

....

....

....

....

DAY 12 – I Am a Child of God

How do you feel knowing that you are a child of God? What qualifies you to be a child of God?

....

....

....

....

....

....

....

....

....

....

....

....

Prayer

Father Lord, I thank you for adopting me into the family of your dear beloved son. Thank you, Holy Spirit, for completing my adoption on my behalf. And thank you for the access given to me to have an intimate fellowship with you, my Lord, and my God. I am very grateful Abba Father.

Exercise: *Take time to write down thoughts, prayers made, prayers answered, gratitude and daily application.*

Day 13: Prayer Requests

....
....
....
....
....
....
....
....
....
....
....
....
....
....
....

DAY 14: Meditation of Scriptures

....
....
....
....
....
....
....
....
....
....
....
....

DAY 15: Reflection

....
....
....
....
....
....
....
....
....
....

Day 16: Application

What are the things that are troubling your heart. Please refer to Luke 11:9

....
....
....
....
....
....
....
....
....
....
....

DAY 17: Prayers Answered

....
....
....
....
....
....
....
....

....

....

....

....

Day 18: Gratitude.

Why are you thankful? Name 5 Things for Which You are Grateful.

....

....

....

....

....

....

....

....

....

....

....

....

....

....

I am a child of God in his family.

Look with wonder at the depth of the Father's marvellous love that he has lavished on us! He has called us and made us his very own beloved children. The reason the world doesn't recognise who we are is that they didn't recognize him. (1 John 3:1 TPT)

Behold, what manner of love the Father has bestowed on you, that you should be called a son of God (1 John 3:1). John wants you to (behold, look at it intensely, and meditate on it) this amazement of the love of God that makes you a child of God. Sometimes, it is pride, and unbelief that makes you not trust the love of God when you see the hurt and pain of life and doubt the love of God, that you are not worthy of it. This is a lie from the pit of hell, the greatness of this love is shown in that by it, you are called a son of God.

And as a child of God, you are a debtor, you are obligated not to live according to the sinful, selfish desires of the flesh. Those who are led by the Spirit of God are the children of God - so, be led by the Spirit. As a believer your self-worth, and self-esteem come from the fact that God loves you and calls you, His children. You are a child of God once you become a born-again Christian - in the now, not in a distant future. Knowing who you are as a child of God makes all the difference and should encourage you to live a fulfilled life -like Jesus did (Romans 8:14-17, Galatians 3:26-27).

As a child of God do not let mercy and truth forsake you, love God and love yourself, it is the value you place on something that equals the amount, others are willing to pay for it. You are valuable to the Father, to this world and to yourself.

DAY 19: Who Calls You a Child of God?

2 Corinthians 6:18, Hebrew 2:11, Romans 8:16

....
....
....
....
....
....
....
....
....
....
....
....

DAY 20 What is it that makes you slow to believe the love of God and that you are a child of God?

....
....
....
....
....
....
....
....

....
....
....
....
....

DAY 21 Do you understand the meaning of being a child of God…

Because not everyone is a child of God (John 1:12) - Why?

....
....
....
....
....
....
....
....
....
....
....
....
....
....

Prayer

Thank you, Father, that I am your child, heir to God and a joint heir to Jesus Christ, my Lord and Saviour.

Thank you for your amazing love, and the Spirit of God that dwell in me.

DAY 22: Prayer Requests

....
....
....
....
....
....
....
....
....
....
....
....

DAY 23: Meditation of Scriptures

....
....
....
....
....

....
....
....
....
....
....

DAY 24: Reflection

....
....
....
....
....
....
....
....
....
....
....
....
....
....
....

DAY 25: Application

What attribute of God do you have and why?

....

....

....

....

....

....

....

....

....

....

....

....

....

....

....

....

....

....

....

....

....

....

DAY 26: Prayers Answered

....
....
....
....
....
....
....
....
....
....
....
....

Day 27: Gratitude.

Why are you thankful? Name 5 Things for Which You are Grateful.

....
....
....
....
....
....
....
....

....
....
....
....
....
....
....
....
....
....
....
....
....
....
....
....
....
....
....

I am a new son, and an appointed seed for this generation (Genesis 4:25 NKJV)

And Adam knew his wife again, and she bore a son and named him [a]Seth, "For God has appointed another seed for me instead of Abel, whom Cain killed."

You have an appointment with God before the foundation of the earth and the appointment is not over until God says so. Do not think your life is over because of the challenges of your past or recent, and the fact that you are still alive, means He is not done with you yet, you have an appointment for a better tomorrow.

After all that Eve had gone through with Cain and Abel, the headaches, experiences, hardship, depression, grief, loss of a son, business, career, house, bankruptcy, and health challenges, she had an appointment with God to have another seed (task) God will never cancel your appointment in His appointment book, He has your name written on His calendar, and have set your destiny. He knows your end from the beginning, He is the author of your life, and He knows what you are going to go through, even now.

The devil knows that God has a plan for you, that is why he is fighting you in every area of your life. He sent trials, tribulations, distractions, lack, and sickness or diseases, to destroy you and if you refused to be destroyed on the outside, he would try even harder to destroy your mind, the battlefield, so be careful to guard your heart, because from it comes the issues of life.

He has come to steal, kill, and destroy but Jesus came to give you, life, and life of abundance (John 10:10) He will never allow the enemy to harm you. Be expectant like a pregnant woman, something good, big, and marvellous is coming your way very soon. Whatever things you have lost, died, or stolen from you in the journey of life, God has another seed for you, a replacement and double for your trouble. When the devil tells you that you are going down, going to die, cave in, or any negative chatters in your mind, tell him that he is a liar and that you know who you are and whose you belong to.

Tell him that you have an appointment with God, you have another seed to give birth to, another miracle for you to hold. Do not give up, you are not at your destination yet. God still has an appointed task for you to finish, look forward to it. Always remember, that you are a son of God, the seed of righteousness, a solider of Christ, a saint, and a servant of the Most-High God. "You Must Never forget who you are and raise your head high when the devil knocks at your door" Selah!!!

Day 28: What appointment do you have with God?

....
....
....
....
....
....
....
....
....
....
....
....
....
....
....
....

DAY 29: You are fully loaded with potential; how do you unleash your potentials?

....
....
....
....
....

....
....
....
....
....
....
....

DAY 30: What new seed have you sow and expecting a result?

....
....
....
....
....
....
....
....
....
....
....
....
....
....
....

DAY 31: Do you believe that God has your name on His calendar for an appointed time?

....

....

....

....

....

....

....

....

....

....

....

....

....

....

....

....

Prayer

Thank you, lord, that I had a pre-set appointment with you before the foundation of the world. Thank you that you have appointed another seed for me; that it is not over with me until, you say so.

DAY 32: Prayer Requests

....
....
....
....
....
....
....
....
....
....
....

DAY 33: Meditation of Scriptures

....
....
....
....
....

....
....
....
....
....
....
....

DAY 34: Reflection

....
....
....
....
....
....
....
....
....
....
....
....
....
....

DAY 35: Application

When is your daily appointed time with God and where/how do you meet with Him?

....

....

....

....

....

....

....

....

....

....

....

DAY 36: Prayers Answered

....

....

....

....

....

....

....

....

....

....

....

....

....

....

....

Day 37: Gratitude.

Why are you thankful? Name 5 Things for Which You are Grateful.

....

....

....

....

....

....

....

....

....

....

....

....

....

....

I am reconciled to God, in Harmony with him.

For if while we were enemies we were reconciled to God through the death of His Son, it is much more certain, having been reconciled, that we will be saved [from the consequences of sin] by His life [that is, we will be saved because Christ lives today]. (Romans 5:10)

While we were yet sinners, Christ died for us to reconcile us back to God, because of His passionate love for us and through the blood of Jesus, we are righteous now. You are the wealth of the glory of God's inheritance. Indeed, you are the hidden treasure in the world.

He chose and reconciled you through the blood of Jesus because you are a pearl of great value. Now you can have and bear abundant life and ask God for provision.

Since you are reconciled to God, you are to release your bitterness, anger, resentment, anxiety, depression, and the need for you to end enmity, animosity, or malice with others. You should be merciful as you endeavour to understand others, be compassionate, show kindness towards others, be patient, humble, gentle, and have perseverance that does not easily take offence with others. God wants a relationship with you, and for you to priorities your time, to spend with Him.

Also, you must ensure that you nurture relationships with others, because building and nurturing relationships can provide support and guidance on the path to your well-being and success. Surrounding yourself with positive, uplifting people who share similar goals, value, and belief can create a network of support system, encouragement, and inspiration. At the same time, invest your effort in fostering meaningful reconciliation, connections and contributing to the well-being of others, which simply means to love your neighbour as yourself.

Day 38: Why did God chose to reconcile you back to Himself through the blood of Jesus?

....
....
....
....
....
....
....
....
....
....
....
....

Day 39: Can you explain what reconciliation means to you?

....
....
....
....
....
....
....
....

....
....
....
....
....
....
....

Day 40: What are some of the consequences of sin and what does grace mean to you?

....
....
....
....
....
....
....
....
....
....
....
....
....
....
....

Day 41: Why were you saved from sin and why are you a pearl of inestimable value?

....

....

....

....

....

....

....

....

....

....

....

....

....

....

....

....

....

....

Prayer

Thank you, Lord, that I am reconciled to God through the death of His son. Thank you for the blood of Jesus that is speaking better things on my behalf, I am grateful Lord, for my identity in Christ.

Day 42: Prayer Requests

....

....

....

....

....

....

....

....

....

....

....

Day 43: Meditation of Scriptures

....

....

....

....

....

....

....

....

....

....

....

....

....

Day 44: Reflection

....

....

....

....

....

....

....

....

....

....

....

....

....

....

....

....

Day 45: Application

Because of the Lord's mercy, you are not consumed (Lamentations 3:22-23)

....

....

....

....

....

....

....

....

....

....

....

Day 46: Prayers Answered

....

....

....

....

....

....

....

....

....

....
....
....
....
....
....

Day 47: Gratitude.

Why are you thankful? Name 5 Things for Which You are Grateful.

....
....
....
....
....
....
....
....
....
....
....
....

I am seen by God as holy, blameless, and above reproach. (Colossians 1:22-23)

Even though you were once distant from him, living in the shadows of your evil thoughts and actions, he reconnected you back to himself. He released his supernatural peace to you through the sacrifice of his own body as the sin-payment on your behalf so that you would dwell in his presence. And now there is nothing between you and Father God, for he sees you as holy, flawless, and restored, if indeed you continue to advance in faith, assured of a firm foundation to grow upon. Never be shaken from the hope of the gospel you have believed in. And this is the glorious news I preach all over the world.

Paul is encouraging you here that as a Christian, you are to advance in faith, and to be on a solid foundation that will make you grow from glory to glory. If you are not growing in your faith, look for a church that speaks the true word of God, that will help you mature because everyone has a measure of faith. Because of Christ's redemption, you are completely forgiven, fully pleasing to God, and totally accepted by God, so robe yourself with virtues of God, since you have been divinely chosen to be holy, blameless, and set apart for glory.

The way you appreciate yourself, your self-esteem, and your self-worth, impacts everything you do, and affects, even the way you pray, study the word of God, and receive the promises of God for your life. If you think you are worthless, nobody with a future, and valueless, you will pray with no power to receive the answer to your prayer, that the promises of God are for others but not for you. God wants you to love and appreciate yourself and your giftings, you are a unique blend of talents, character, and giftings and have a phenomenal destiny!!! You are good, and you are somebody great.

Day 48: Why are you seen by God as holy, blameless, and above reproach?

....
....
....
....
....
....
....
....
....
....
....
....

Day 49: How do you feel, knowing that God has reconnected you back to Himself?

....
....
....
....
....
....
....

....
....
....
....
....
....
....
....

Day 50: What are the things that you need to do, to grow your faith?

....
....
....
....
....
....
....
....
....
....
....
....
....
....

Prayer

Father Lord, thank you for reconnecting me to Yourself. Jesus, I pray for myself and my friends who still affirm the gospel, but who feel disconnected from your presence and like strangers to your love and struggling with identity crises, Please Lord, renew, refresh, and restore us, as you help us to grow in our faith. Thank you, Lord.

Day 51: Prayer Requests

....
....
....
....
....
....
....
....
....
....
....
....
....

Day 52: Meditation of Scriptures

....
....
....
....

....

....

....

....

....

....

....

....

....

....

Day 53: Reflection

....

....

....

....

....

....

....

....

....

....

....

....

....

....

Day 54: Application

Is God gracious and compassionate? Why? Psalm 145:8

....
....
....
....
....
....
....
....
....
....
....

Day 55: Prayers Answered

....
....
....
....
....
....
....
....
....

....
....
....
....
....
....

Day 56: Gratitude.

Why are you thankful? Name 5 Things for Which You are Grateful.

....
....
....
....
....
....
....
....
....
....
....
....
....
....

I am sealed with God's Holy Spirit. (Ephesians 1:13 AMP)

In Him, you also, when you heard the word of truth, the good news of your salvation, and [as a result] believed in Him, were stamped with the seal of the promised Holy Spirit [the One promised by Christ] as owned *and* protected [by God].

When you heard and believed in Jesus, and the moment you put your trust in Him, you were sealed with the promise of the Holy Spirit that reside inside of you. What a wonderful, glorious God, who did not only forgive you of your sins but also sealed you with the Holy Spirit and who is the guarantor of your inheritance. The word seal means "a device or substance that is used to join two things together so as to prevent them from coming apart or to prevent anything from passing between them" this is exactly how you are glued to the Holy spirit, so that no enemy can penetrate or come between you and the Holy Spirit.

You were sealed means God's approval of you as His child, mark of ownership is upon your forehead, glued, and engraved by the blood of Jesus. The seal of the Holy Spirit is to certify that you are special, secured from all evil, as a guarantor for your salvation, and to indicate the authenticity of your identity in Christ Jesus. Always remember, that you have the mark of the precious blood of Jesus upon you, so fear not, you are carried with the protection and provision of your owner, God. The blood of Jesus is a guarantee that you have been redeemed, bought at full price, and sealed with the Holy Spirit and you can do all things through Christ Jesus

Someone with a healthy self-concept will experience the pain of failure and defeat there would not be damages done by it, someone with a positive sense of self-esteem can enjoy personal strength and tolerate the awareness of weakness is. This is a wholesome love for oneself. Do you love yourself this way? Do you enjoy being you?

God has blessed you with every spiritual blessing, choosing you, declares you holy and blameless, adopted you, redeemed you, forgiving you, made known to you, the mystery of his will, and sealed you with Holy Spirit.

Day 57: What is your assurance that you are sealed with the Holy Spirit?

....
....
....
....
....
....
....
....
....
....

Day 58: How did you hear about Jesus and accepted Him as your Lord and saviour?

....
....
....
....
....
....
....
....

....

....

....

....

Day 59: Do you have a personal relationship with the Holy Spirit? If not Why?

....

....

....

....

....

....

....

....

....

....

....

....

....

....

Prayer

I am so grateful that I am sealed with the Holy Spirit, the moment I received Jesus Christ as my Lord and Saviour. I pray that nothing will come between me and the Holy Spirit, and God will not take the Holy Spirit away from me. Thank you, Abba Father.

Day 60: Prayer Requests

....
....
....
....
....
....
....
....
....
....
....

Day 61: Meditation of Scriptures

....
....
....
....
....
....

....
....
....
....
....
....
....

Day 62: Reflections

....
....
....
....
....
....
....
....
....
....
....
....
....
....
....

Day 63: Application

How do you demonstrate your relationship with the Holy Spirit? 1 Corinthians 14:15

....
....
....
....
....
....
....
....
....
....
....
....

Day 64: Prayers Answered

....
....
....
....
....
....
....
....
....

....
....
....
....
....
....
....

Day 65: Gratitude.

Why are you thankful? Name 5 Things for Which You are Grateful.

....
....
....
....
....
....
....
....
....
....
....
....
....

I am called to accomplish God's purpose. Romans 8:28-30

And we know [with great confidence] that God [who is deeply concerned about us] causes all things to work together [as a plan] for good for those who love God, to those who are called according to His plan and purpose. For those whom He foreknew [and loved and chose beforehand], He also predestined to be conformed to the image of His Son [and ultimately share in His complete sanctification], so that He would be the firstborn [the most beloved and honoured] among many believers. And those whom He predestined, He also called; and those whom He called, He also justified [declared free of the guilt of sin]; and those whom He justified, He also glorified [raising them to a heavenly dignity].

All the things that happen to you in the journey of life, even the bad ones, God usually turn it around for your good. Every detail of your life is carefully woven together for your good and for those who are called according to His purpose.

When God calls you, He justifies you, by given you freedom from sin, and those whom He justifies, He glorified for His glory. Because of Christ redemption, you are worthy, forgiven, loved, accepted and complete in Him. (Colossians: 2:10) Paul made it clear that we are complete through Christ alone, nothing else.

"By striving to find completeness through any other source, such as success, approval and opinions of others, prestige, fame or appearance is to be taken captive through philosophy and empty deception (Colossians 2:8) nothing can add to the death of Christ to pay for your sins and the resurrection of Christ to give us new life."

Day 66: What qualifies you to be complete in Christ Jesus and how does this make you feel?

....

....

....

....

....

....

....

....

....

....

....

....

....

Day 67: How is the feeling of being unqualify stops you from your calling?

....

....

....

....

....

....

....

....

....

....

....
....
....
....
....
....

Day 68: Do you think you are qualified for God's calling and justification?

....
....
....
....
....
....
....
....
....
....
....
....
....
....
....
....
....

Day 69: Where do you feel or think God is leading you to in this season?

....
....
....
....
....
....
....
....
....
....
....
....
....
....
....
....
....
....

Prayer

Lord Jesus, I come with joy and confidence to the occupied throne of grace today, to thank you for all that you have done for me, and for giving me a secure identity.

Day 70: Prayer Requests

....
....
....
....
....
....
....
....
....
....
....

Day 71: Meditation of Scripture

....
....
....
....
....
....
....
....

....
....
....

Day 72: Reflection

....
....
....
....
....
....
....
....
....
....
....
....

Day 73: Application

What do you understand by those He called, He justified and glorified.

....
....
....
....
....
....

....
....
....
....
....
....
....
....

Day 74: Prayers Answered.

....
....
....
....
....
....
....
....
....
....
....
....
....
....
....
....

Day 75: Gratitude

Why are you thankful? Name 5 Things for Which You are Grateful.

....
....
....
....
....
....
....
....
....
....
....
....
....
....
....
....
....

I am a full Citizen among God's people (Ephesians 2:19)

So, then you are no longer strangers and aliens [outsiders without rights of citizenship], but you are fellow citizens with the saints (God's people) and are [members] of God's household.

What an awesome peace you have knowing that you are a heavenly citizen, amongst the children of God. No matter what you are going through in life, have that consciousness that you are not a stranger or a child without rights of citizenship, but you can now come boldly to the throne of grace and speak to your heavenly Father just like any other man or woman of God.

So, you are not foreigners or guests, but rather you are one of the children of the city of the holy ones, with all the rights as family member. As a full citizen of heaven, you are to enjoy all the benefits that come with your citizenship. You must desire the goodness of the Lord in the land of the living and all the fullness of God upon your life.

Heavenly citizens do not lack any good thing; thus, you should not lack because you spend from the pocket of Jehovah, your great provider. You should be like the sons of Issachar, who understand the time and knew what Israel should do. *[NB: The bible refers to a people who would do things differently based on the seasons as they changed – they were called children / Sons of Issachar]*

To Ponder:

Do you know the season in which you are now?

Do you know that you are a solution provider in this generation?

The world is waiting for you to solve a problem they have; and you are the one with the solution. So, do get up from your comfort zone and get going -so that men see your good works and glorify God, your father in heaven through you.

Know that you are complete because Christ has forgiven you and given you abundance life, peace, joy of the Holy Ghost and the capacity for growth, transformation, and change.

Day 76: How do you feel, knowing that you are a heavenly citizen?

....
....
....
....
....
....
....
....
....
....
....

Day 77: Citizen vs a Foreigner / an Alien

What do you understand by a foreigner or an alien? Notice: this is who you used to be.

....
....
....
....
....
....
....

....

....

....

....

....

Day 78: Being a Citizen of Heaven

In what way do you struggle to believe the truth that you are now a citizen of heaven.

....

....

....

....

....

....

....

....

....

....

....

....

....

....

....

....

....

Prayer

Lord, I thank you for making me a full citizen among God's people.

Please Lord, give me the eyes to see myself, the way you see me, in Jesus Name.

Day 79: Prayer Requests

....
....
....
....
....
....
....
....
....
....

Day 80: Meditation of Scriptures

....
....
....
....
....
....
....
....

....

....

....

....

....

....

Day 81: Reflection

....

....

....

....

....

....

....

....

....

....

....

....

....

....

....

....

Day 82: Application

How do you embrace your uniqueness? And how proud are you to be a citizen of Heaven?

....

....

....

....

....

....

....

....

....

....

....

....

Day 83: Prayers Answered

....

....

....

....

....

....

....

....

....
....
....
....
....
....
....

Day 84: Gratitude

Why You Are Thankful? Name 5 Things for Which You are Grateful.

....
....
....
....
....
....
....
....
....
....
....
....
....

I am justified, declared right in God's sight. (Romans 5:1)

Therefore, since we have been justified [that is, acquitted of sin, declared blameless before God] by faith, [let us grasp the fact that] we have peace with God [and the joy of reconciliation with Him] through our Lord Jesus Christ (the Messiah, the Anointed).

We are justified by faith. Justified means to be proven just or right, so you are proven righteous by faith.

Because you are justified in His sight, you have a free, abundant, and immediate access to God.

You are unstoppable in every area of your life, and no enemy can hold you back from being the best in God's assignment of God for your life.

He becomes your refuge and your fortress. And you who was once alienated and enemy in mind by wicked works, yet now He has reconciled you in His body of His flesh through death, to present you Holy and blameless above reproach in His sight.

What a wonderful, awesome father, you have.

When your faith is completely intact in Jesus, you are made right in the sight of God, and the peace that passes all understanding comes from placing faith in God. Knowing and experiencing this truth becomes more real as you understand that you are loved and forgiven of all your sins, and God opens a clean slate for you, just as you put your trust in Jesus Christ and God sees you as a brand-new creature and made right before Him.

Your faith and hope in Christ help you to endure during trials or tribulations in life.

That suffering which you are going through or have been through prunes your character, and teaches one patience, and perseverance.

Therefore, since we have been made right in God's sight by faith, we have peace with God because of what Jesus Christ our Lord has done for us. (Romans 5:1 NLT)

So, dive into the love of God and allow the peace of God to subdue all your fears, because God has not given you the spirit of fear. Scripture says that God has given His children:

…but a Spirit of power, love, and of sound mind.

Please remember that your righteousness (right standing) is in Christ Jesus

Day 85: Justified by Faith in Christ

How do you feel about being justified, and being declared as in *right standing*, in God's sight?

....
....
....
....
....
....
....
....
....
....
....
....
....

Day 86: The Justified Life

What benefits do you enjoyed as you have been justified?

....
....
....
....
....
....
....

....

....

....

....

....

....

....

Day 87: Free Access to God

Do you know that you have free, abundant, and immediate access to God?

How often do you use this access?

....

....

....

....

....

....

....

....

....

....

....

....

Prayer

Thank you for justifying and declaring me right in your sight. Thank you, Lord for the free access to your throne of grace.

Day 88: Prayer Requests

....
....
....
....
....
....
....
....
....
....
....

Day 89: Meditation of Scriptures

....
....
....
....
....
....
....
....

....
....
....
....
....
....
....
....

Day 90: Reflection

....
....
....
....
....
....
....
....
....
....
....
....
....
....
....
....
....

Day 91: Application

How would you demonstrate love to those who offended you?

....
....
....
....
....
....
....
....
....
....
....
....

Day 92: Prayers Answered

....
....
....
....
....
....
....
....
....

....
....
....
....

Day 93: Gratitude

Why are you thankful? Name 5 Things for Which You are Grateful.

....
....
....
....
....
....
....
....
....
....
....
....

I am sanctified, set apart by God's spirit. (1 Corinthians 6:11)

But you were washed [by the atoning sacrifice of Christ], you were sanctified [set apart for God, and made holy], you were justified [declared free of guilt] in the name of the Lord Jesus Christ and in the [Holy] Spirit of our God [the source of the believer's new life and changed behaviour]. God is faithful and forgiving.

We were all once sinners, doing bad things that upset God. Through the blood of Jesus is forgiveness. As we accept Jesus to be our Lord and saviour, God in His mercy and grace sanctifies and sets us apart, by His Spirit and for His glory and purposes.

Understand this, that God desires all your heart, if you have sinned, repent now, and receive His free gift of salvation. He promises and forgives us; you and I of all our sin…

No matter the guilt you are facing because of your sin, cast all your trouble, anxiety, mental health, emptiness, lack of fruitfulness/ barrenness… at His feet now and be free.

Do not pick any of your past issues up again, do not look back, but focus on God who is able to restore all things to you and even more.

When God created man, he gave him a sense of purpose. When men rebelled against God, he lost that God giving sense of significance since then he has tried to find purpose and meaning apart from God. But God has made us in such a way that he is the only one he's who can meet our needs. Money fame, find homes, sport cars material things, prestige, in each profession are only counterfeits of the true significance we have in Christ. By this counterfeit promise to meet our needs for fulfilments, that which they accumulate never last. God's purpose for your life, is the only thing that can give you a long-lasting sense of significance.

You may feel better, because of your achievements or even Christian activities, devotional time, prayer, witnessing, Bible studies, church attendance. failure to meet your standards, and all others in any area can cause you to feel poorly about yourself.

Jesus is the answer, give it to God just trust God and it really worked out just pray about it. Praise God, for His wonderful love.

Day 94: What do you understand sanctified, justified and forgiveness?

....
....
....
....
....
....
....
....
....
....
....
....

Day 95: I Am Forgiven

Do you believe that God has forgiven you of your sin?

....
....
....
....
....
....
....

....

....

....

....

....

....

....

....

....

....

....

....

....

....

....

....

....

Prayer

Thank you, Lord, that I am sanctified and set apart for your glory. Thank you for declaring me free from all guilt and giving me the Holy Spirit.

Day 96: What does Mercy and Grace mean to you?

....
....
....
....
....
....
....
....
....
....
....

Day 97: Prayer Requests

....
....
....
....
....
....
....

....
....
....
....
....

Day 98: Meditation of Scriptures

....
....
....
....
....
....
....
....
....
....
....
....

Day 99: Reflection

....
....
....
....
....

....

....

....

....

....

....

....

....

....

....

....

Congratulations! *...for commitment and disciplined till Day 99.*

Consider what this Journey has done for you! Congratulations

Day 100: Application of Forgiveness:

How do you deal with heavy burdens in your heart, caused by sinful decisions?

Have you taken this to God and asked for forgiveness?

....

....

....

....

....

....

....

....

....

....

....

....

Day 101: Prayers Answered

....

....

....

....

....

....

....

....

....
....
....
....
....
....

Day 102: Gratitude

Why are you thankful? Name 5 Things for Which You are Grateful.

....
....
....
....
....
....
....
....
....
....
....
....
....

I am redeemed, bought with Christ's blood. (Ephesians 1:7)

Since we are now joined to Christ, we have been given the treasures of redemption by his blood—the total cancellation of our sins—all because of the cascading riches of his grace.

What a wonderful news to know that you have been redeemed and bought by the precious blood of Jesus.

Notice…You are the one that committed sin, you are the one worthy of death penalty, but God sent His only begotten Son, who was sinless to take your place on the cross. God loves you and wants to forgive you of every sin that you commit.

What manner of love is this, that made God to deliver His son for your transgression, while you were set free and free indeed.

When Jesus said it is finished, He meant that He has made full payment for your sin, "through his blood." Paul is referring to Christ's death on the cross as the sufficient payment for the sins of all who believe and have released you from the eternal penalty and the earthly power of our sins. It is only in Christ that you have redemption through his blood" (1:7).

Redemption means buying someone out of slavery or, more importantly, freeing someone from some sort of bondage, which means you are no longer a slave to sin or fear but you are now a child of God.

The enemy, addiction, fear, mental health issues, sickness, guilt, pain, and lack have no power over you, anymore.

The blood of Jesus has the purchasing power, to do and undo everything contrary to the will of God in your life, and not only to obtain but also to cleanse you, wash, sanctify, and make you righteous and holy before God. You must remember that heaven does not deal in dollars, pounds, euros, or even gold or silver but the blood of Jesus that speaks better things on your behalf.

Day 103: Redemption

What does it mean to be redeemed? What are the benefits?

....
....
....
....
....
....
....
....
....
....
....
....

Day 104: Have you ever asked God to forgive you of your sin?

....
....
....
....
....
....
....
....

....

....

....

....

Day 105: Can you describe the Love of God towards you; can you measure His Love?

....

....

....

....

....

....

....

....

....

....

....

....

....

....

....

....

Prayer

Father thank you for sending your beloved Son to die for my sin. Thank you for redeeming and buying me back with His precious blood.

Day 106: Prayer Requests

....
....
....
....
....
....
....
....
....
....

Day 107: Meditation of Scriptures

....
....
....
....
....
....
....
....

....

....

....

....

....

....

....

Day 108: Reflection

....

....

....

....

....

....

....

....

....

....

....

....

....

....

Day 109: Application

How do you forgive others their trespasses (sin)?

....

....

....

....

....

....

....

....

....

....

....

....

....

Day 110: Prayers Answered

....

....

....

....

....

....

....

....

....
....
....
....
....

Day 111: Gratitude

Why are you thankful? Name 5 Things for Which You are Grateful.

....
....
....
....
....
....
....
....
....
....
....
....
....
....

I am cleansed by Christ's blood for all my sins (1 John 1:7)

but if we [really] walk in the Light [that is, live each and every day in conformity with the precepts of God], as He Himself is in the Light, we have [true, unbroken] fellowship with one another [He with us, and we with Him], and the blood of Jesus His Son cleanses us from all sin [by erasing the stain of sin, keeping us cleansed from sin in all its forms and manifestations].

You are cleansed by the blood of Jesus from all your sin. You are starting on a clean slate, do not remember, the former things nor consider the things of old, for God is doing a new thing for you. Because of what Jesus had done for you, you are now walking in divine favour with God and with man, and favour surrounds you like a shield, you are honoured and special to God. You are justified by the blood of Jesus, so you are no longer a slave to fear, anger, low self-esteem, anxiety, and depression. No obstacle can stop you; no hindrance can delay you, and your pathway is caved for abundance, multiplication, good health, goodness, mercy, wealth and all-round favour with God and man.

Day 112: What do you understand by being cleansed by the blood of Jesus?

....
....
....
....
....
....
....
....
....
....
....
....

Day 113: Do you feel that you are special to God, why?

....
....
....
....
....
....
....
....

....

....

....

....

....

....

....

Day 114: What Kind Of Relationship Do You Have With Jesus Christ?

....

....

....

....

....

....

....

....

....

....

....

....

....

....

Day 115: Prayer Requests

....

....

....

....

....

....

....

....

....

....

....

....

....

....

....

....

Prayer

Lord thank you for cleansing me from all unrighteousness.

Lord, help me to conform to you daily, to listen to your still voice, and to love you more and more. Thank you for hearing my prayer.

Day 116: Meditation of Scriptures

....

....

....

....

....

....

....

....

....

....

Day 117: Reflection

....

....

....

....

....

....

....

....
....
....
....
....
....

Day 118: Application

Where are you walking as a light of the world?

....
....
....
....
....
....
....
....
....
....
....
....
....
....
....

Day 119: Prayers Answered

....
....
....
....
....
....
....
....
....
....
....
....
....

Day 120: Gratitude

Why are you thankful? Name 5 Things for Which You are Grateful.

....
....
....
....
....
....
....
....

....

....

....

....

....

....

....

....

....

....

....

....

....

....

....

....

....

....

....

....

I am heir of God, and the joint heir with Christ. (Romans 8:16-17)

The Spirit Himself testifies and confirms together with our spirit [assuring us] that we [believers] are children of God. And if [we are His] children, [then we are His] heirs also: heirs of God and fellow heirs with Christ [sharing His spiritual blessing and inheritance], if indeed we share in His suffering so that we may also share in His glory.

It is an offense (consider it as an insult, so to say)... to know that people always hunger for what they already are. The bible says you are heir to God, which means, you are a very important heir apparent to the heavenly throne, you have an automatic right to legally receive all or most of the inheritances of your Father God. God loves you so much that He made you to be joint heir with Jesus Christ. What an awesome father that leaves the 99 sheep to go and search for one lost sheep. He cares for you and if you were the only one on earth, He would have still died for you, because of His love for us all.

Day 121: How do you feel, knowing that you are an heir of God?

....
....
....
....
....
....
....
....
....
....
....
....
....

Day 122: How do you know that God loves you?

....
....
....
....
....
....
....
....

....
....
....
....
....
....
....
....

Day 123: In your own words describe Grace, what is Grace to you?

....
....
....
....
....
....
....
....
....
....
....
....
....
....

Prayer

Lord thank you for loving me to the extent of making me a partaker of the kingdom.

I am very grateful to be your heir and joint heir to Christ Jesus. Thank you, Lord.

Day 124: Prayer Requests

....
....
....
....
....
....
....
....
....
....

Day 125: Meditation of Scriptures

....
....
....
....
....
....

....
....
....
....
....

Day 126: Reflection

....
....
....
....
....
....
....
....
....
....
....
....

Day 127: Application

How do you tell others about the love of God?

....
....
....
....
....

....
....
....
....
....
....
....
....
....

Day 128: Prayers Answered

....
....
....
....
....
....
....
....
....
....
....
....
....

Day 129: Gratitude

Why are you thankful? Name 5 Things for Which You are Grateful.

....

....

....

....

....

....

....

....

....

....

....

....

....

....

....

....

....

....

I am complete in Christ (Colossians 2:10)

And in Him you have been made complete [achieving spiritual stature through Christ], and He is the head over all rule and authority [of every angelic and earthly power].

"The word "complete" in Greek signifies being made full, and the word "you" is plural. It is speaking to all who are in Christ. The order of the wording in Greek gives us the idea of what is being relayed – "And you are in Him, made full." You are complete in Christ Jesus because of what he has done for you on the cross.

Complete simply means wholeness, to be full, to lack none of the parts, to lack nothing. You have every part in Christ as a member of His body, and all that you need to fulfil your purpose and your destiny, you are complete (perfect) in Him to help you stand before the throne of grace as Jesus Christ is standing at God's right hand and to be complete in Jesus also means whole in your body, mind, soul, and spirit-filled satisfying Christ. Jesus came to set you free from sin and made you brand new through the blood of Jesus.

God is your portion. He is a part of your wholeness, and Jesus came for the totality, entire of you without continuation. You are complete in Him which is the head of all principality and power. In Christ Jesus you are complete and without Him, you are not complete. Jesus is the beginning and the end, the Alpha and Omega of your life.

Therefore, you should stop looking for wholeness in the wrong places like in materialism, success, relationships, addictions, career, money, and validation from others. You are to realise that nothing else except God has the power to complete you, then stop expecting unrealistic promises from others, and rely on God alone for all your needs, healing, and significance. And above all, seek first the kingdom of God and its righteousness, then all other things shall be added unto it, do not live your life pleasing others but seek God by discovering and fulfilling your purpose.

Day 130: What do you understand by being complete in Christ?

....

....

....

....

....

....

....

....

....

....

....

....

....

Day 131: What are the benefits of being complete in Christ Jesus?

....

....

....

....

....

....

....

....

....
....
....
....
....

Day 132: What do you understand that you are incomplete without Jesus?

....
....
....
....
....
....
....
....
....
....
....
....
....
....

Prayer

Lord thank you for making me to be fully complete in Christ Jesus. I thank you that nothing else can satisfy me or complete me but you Lord.

Day 133: Prayer Requests

....

....

....

....

....

....

....

....

....

....

....

....

Day 134: Meditation of Scripture

....

....

....

....

....

....

....
....
....
....
....
....

Day 135: Reflection

....
....
....
....
....
....
....
....
....
....
....
....
....
....
....
....
....
....

Day 136: Application

How do you behave and act, knowing that you are complete in Christ Jesus?

....

....

....

....

....

....

....

....

....

....

....

....

Day 137: Prayers Answered

....

....

....

....

....

....

....

....
....
....
....
....
....
....

Day 138: Gratitude

Why are you thankful? Name 5 Things for Which You are Grateful.

....
....
....
....
....
....
....
....
....
....
....
....

I am an ambassador for Christ. (2 Corinth.5:20)

We are ambassadors of the Anointed One who carry the message of Christ to the world, as though God were tenderly pleading with them directly through our lips. So, we tenderly plead with you on Christ's behalf, "Turn back to God and be reconciled to him."

When you are an ambassador, you are a representation of your home country, and all your welfare is taken care of by your country, so you are God's representative here on earth, and

He will supply all your needs according to His riches in glory through Christ Jesus. You are protected from every harm, as your needs are met, and you take instructions from your home country, although you obey the rules and policies of your host country, your allegiance is to your home country. As good ambassadors who represent their countries, you must understand your country's rules and regulations, foreign and economic international policy, and would aggressively defend these policies in the country that you are posted to, just as you are expected to boldly defend the word of God and not to conform to the world or things of the world.

Day 139: How do you feel being an ambassador of Jesus Christ?

....
....
....
....
....
....
....
....
....
....
....
....
....

Day 140: What are your roles as an ambassador?

....
....
....
....
....
....
....
....
....

....

....

....

....

....

....

....

....

....

....

Day 141: As an ambassador of Christ, how willing are you to represent Him in the world.

....

....

....

....

....

....

....

....

....

....

....

....

Prayer

Thank you, Lord, for choosing me to be your ambassador here on earth. Thank you for watching over me, protection and for my daily provision.

Day 142: Prayer Requests

....
....
....
....
....
....
....
....
....
....
....
....

Day 143: Meditation of Scriptures

....
....
....
....
....
....

....
....
....
....
....
....
....

Day 144: Reflection

....
....
....
....
....
....
....
....
....
....
....
....
....
....
....
....

Day 145: Application

How do you carry out your duties as an ambassador and list them?

....

....

....

....

....

....

....

....

....

....

....

....

Day 146: Prayers Answered

....

....

....

....

....

....

....

....

....

....

....

....

Day 147: Gratitude

Why are you thankful? Name 5 Things for Which You are Grateful.

....

....

....

....

....

....

....

....

....

....

....

....

....

....

....

....

I am being conformed to the character of Christ. (Romans 8:29)

For he knew all about us before we were born, and he destined us from the beginning to share the likeness of his Son. This means the Son is the oldest among a vast family of brothers and sisters who will become just like him.

God is saying to you, that He knew you before you were formed in the womb, before you were known by anyone else, He knew who you are, who you would become, your destiny, purpose, and your destination in life. He specially made you in His image and His likeness. He is the potter, and you are the clay, a potter can make a pot, and in the process, if he decides to break the pot, he can remould it again to his specification. So, God made you to be conformed to the character of Jesus, to be His heir and a joint heir to Jesus Christ. For you to conform to Christ, you need the fruit of the Holy Spirit to compliment the character of Jesus which are love, joy, peace, endurance, kindness, goodness, faithfulness, gentleness, and self-control.

Day 148: How do you feel being conformed to the character of Christ?

....

....

....

....

....

....

....

....

....

....

....

....

....

....

Day 149: Name some of the character of Jesus Christ?

....

....

....

....

....

....

....

....

....

....

....

....

....

....

....

....

....

Day 150: Which of the fruit of the Spirit do you need to work on, or you desire to have?

....

....

....

....

....

....

....

....

....

....

....

....

....

Prayer

Thank you, Abba Father for conforming me to the character of Christ, Lord, give me the grace to have the fruit of the Spirit and to have what you have as a joint heir of the father.

Day 151: Prayer Requests

....
....
....
....
....
....
....
....
....
....
....

Day 152: Meditation of Scriptures

....
....
....
....
....
....

....

....

....

....

....

....

Day 153: Reflection

....

....

....

....

....

....

....

....

....

....

....

....

....

....

....

Day 154: Application

How do you desire the Fruit of the Spirit and what do you need to do?

....
....
....
....
....
....
....
....
....
....
....

Day 155: Prayers Answered

....
....
....
....
....
....
....
....
....

....

....

....

....

....

Day 156: Gratitude

Why are you thankful? Name 5 Things for Which You are Grateful.

....

....

....

....

....

....

....

....

....

....

....

....

....

I am Treasured (Colossians 3:3)

For you died [to this world], and your [new, real] life is hidden with Christ in God.

You are hidden in Christ, and because you are hidden in Christ, you become untouchable, which means you wear a designer label that says touch not my anointing and do my prophet no harm. You are precious, a diamond and a special jewel. You do not see the diamond, everywhere, it is hidden in the soil until it is dug out, and when it is raw, no one desires it until it goes through a process, after that it becomes state-of-the-art for display. This is how God will display you before kings, that when men see your light, they will glorify your Father in Heaven.

You are a seed untapped, just as you are hidden in Christ, so your potentials are hidden inside of you until you unlock them, you will not shine like a diamond and be valuable before men. So, learn to unleash your potential, which means to release all your gifts, talent, creativity, and ideals that are hidden within you. The moment you tap into your potential by faith, you will be surprised by what you can do, and then your light will shine for the whole world to see and glorify your Father in Heaven.

You must allow anybody to influence you, be who God created you to be and know whose you are. Your limitation does not define who you are, you are not in competition with anybody, if you want to maximise who you are in life, you do not tell story about what has happened to you in the past, but you should ask this question, what will I do to come out of this situation? Then you will find the solution to your problem.

Day 157: What does the word treasured means to you and do you feel hidden in Christ?

....

....

....

....

....

....

....

....

....

....

....

....

Day 158: What are the qualities of a diamond?

....

....

....

....

....

....

....

....

....
....
....
....
....
....
....

Day 159: what does it mean to die to the world?

....
....
....
....
....
....
....
....
....
....
....
....
....
....
....
....

Day 160: What area of your life, have you gone through a process that is painful?

....

....

....

....

....

....

....

....

....

....

....

....

....

....

....

....

....

....

Prayer

Thank you, Lord, for you are the all-knowing God, who knows me and accept me, just as I am. Thank you for the designer label that I wear always, which makes me unique and different from others.

Day 161: Prayer Requests

....

....

....

....

....

....

....

....

....

....

....

Day 162: Meditation of Scriptures

....

....

....

....

....

....

....

....

....

....

....

Day 163: Reflection

....

....

....

....

....

....

....

....

....

....

....

....

Day 164: Application

How do you apply Colossians 3:3 to your life and others?

....

....

....

....

....

....

....

....

....

....

....

....

Day 165: Prayers Answered

....

....

....

....

....

....

....

....

....

....

....

....

....

....

Day 166: Gratitude

Why are you thankful? Name 5 Things for Which You are Grateful.

....

....

....

....

....

....

....

....

....

....

....

....

....

....

....

....

....

I am Valuable and a God's special creation (Psalm 139: 13-14)

For You formed my innermost parts; You knit me [together] in my mother's womb. I will give thanks and praise to You, for I am fearfully and wonderfully made; Wonderful are Your works, and my soul knows it very well.

You are valuable to God, your Heavenly Father. You see, you are not a random fluke of genetics or evolution. by Charles Darwin. Would you let this truth define who you are and the way you see yourself today? And continue to say this to yourself, I am God's special creation. You are a one-of-a-kind creation by the Creator and superbly crafted for His use and glory. You are hand-stitched and custom-tailored, and you have been carefully conceived and constructed to fit God's purpose on earth.

You are made in God's image; you should have His characteristics as His child and let the world know this as you represent God wherever you are by your good works and acts of kindness. God chose every aspect of your personality, crafted every gift and talent, He bestowed on you, and gave special thought to each of your features and traits. He custom-designed you to fit a specific role in His sovereign plan for the world and you are a designer original. Your fingerprint, hand, voice, footprint, and total genetic code are different from any other person, living or dead.

You are a diamond, a rose, and a jewel, a special species and you are a precious stone, purchased by the blood of Jesus Christ. In the eyes of God, you are worth dying for, you are incomparable, and stop comparing yourself with others (2 Corinthians 10:12), if not you allow doubt, low self-esteem, and limiting beliefs to set into your mind. Then you will start to say I am not good enough, I am not as gifted or talented as the other person, I cannot do it, I am not as beautiful as others, my life is hard or tied of life. All these negative words become a self-fulfilling prophecy. Comparison destroys confidence and limits you from your purpose. Nobody has the same experience, talent, personality, strengths and weaknesses, abilities, disabilities, skills, training, and connections as you.

Always remember, that you are fearfully and wonderfully made, and know that your circumstances or situation will Never change who you are and who you are.

Day 167: Do you feel or know that you are fearfully and wonderfully Made by God?

....

....

....

....

....

....

....

....

....

....

....

....

....

Day 168: What are the deep things in your heart, you think God does not understand?

....

....

....

....

....

....

....

....

....
....
....
....
....
....

Day 169: How has comparison affected your courageous and limit you?

....
....
....
....
....
....
....
....
....
....
....
....
....
....

Day 170: What do you understand by "you knitted me together in my mother's womb"?

....

....

....

....

....

....

....

....

....

....

....

....

....

....

....

....

Prayer

Lord I am so grateful, that I am fearfully and wonderfully made by you. Thank you that you knew me before anyone else and you set me apart for your glory.

Day 171: Prayer Requests

....
....
....
....
....
....
....
....
....
....

Day 172: Meditation of Scriptures

....
....
....
....
....
....

....
....
....
....
....
....
....

Day 173: Reflection

....
....
....
....
....
....
....
....
....
....
....
....
....
....
....
....

Day 174: Application

What are some of the advantages of God knowing everything about you?

....
....
....
....
....
....
....
....
....
....
....

Day 175: Prayers Answered

....
....
....
....
....
....
....
....

....

....

....

....

Day 176: Gratitude

Why are you thankful? Name 5 Things for Which You are Grateful.

....

....

....

....

....

....

....

....

....

....

....

....

....

....

You are a chosen Race, King, and a Priest (1 Peter 2:9)

But you are a chosen race, a royal Priesthood, a consecrated Nation, a [special] PEOPLE FOR *God's* OWN POSSESSION, so that you may proclaim the excellences [the wonderful deeds and virtues and perfections] of Him who called you out of darkness into His marvellous light.

God hand-picked you out of the millions of sperms, while others perished, you were chosen by Him, made you a king to rule and reign of earth, consecrated you, and anointed you a priest, and king. You are not common nor ordinary, you are royalty, holy, and included with those God calls His possession.

He protected you from harm, shielded and covered you for His glory. God loves you so much that He allowed righteousness to go before you and make His footsteps, your pathways so that you will not stumble your feet against any stone. God is seeking your attention, through some of the challenges, circumstances, or troubles of life. He said to draw near to me, and I will draw near to you.

The issues of the past are a training ground for your promotion and lifting, just like the story of Joseph, who was betrayed by his brothers, sold into slavery, went into prison, and from prison to the palace, and God was with him all through the process just as God is with you now in that situation that you are passing through. You are where you are for a specific and special reason. As a light of the world, let your light so shine before men, that they will glorify your father in heaven. The host of heaven is cheering you up, do not give up. You are needed for such a time as this.

Day 177: Identity

Which one of the four truths about the identity of Christ followers do you know you are?

....

....

....

....

....

....

....

....

....

....

....

....

Day 178: How does any of the descriptions shape your life or the way you view God?

....

....

....

....

....

....

....

....
....
....
....
....
....
....
....

Day 179: How do you feel as a special people of God's own possession?

....
....
....
....
....
....
....
....
....
....
....
....
....
....

Day 180: Chosen Race

Do you know who you are as a chosen generation, royal Priesthood and Holy Nation?

.

Prayer

Lord, thank you that I am chosen, a royal priesthood, and a holy nation onto you. I am valuable and significant because of you. Thank you, Father, that you will realign me to my purpose and destiny.

Day 181: Prayer Requests

....

....

....

....

....

....

....

....

....

....

Day 182: Meditation of Scriptures

....

....

....

....

....

....

....

....
....
....
....
....
....
....
....

Day 183: Reflection

....
....
....
....
....
....
....
....
....
....
....
....
....
....
....
....

Day 184: Application

In what way were you in darkness before you became a believer? Why is it hard for you to abstain from sinful desires?

....
....
....
....
....
....
....
....
....
....
....
....

Day 185: Prayers Answered

....
....
....
....
....
....
....
....

....

....

....

....

....

Day 186: Gratitude

Why are you thankful? Name 5 Things for Which You are Grateful.

....

....

....

....

....

....

....

....

....

....

....

....

....

....

....

I am important to God (Psalm 100:3)

Know (perceive, recognise, and understand with approval) that the Lord is God! It is He Who has made us, not we ourselves [and we are His]! We are His people and the sheep of His pasture.

God made you out of the dust, but when He breathe upon you, you became His image with everything you needed to live and survived throughout your lifetime. As sheep is important to a shepherd, which makes him to leave the 99, and go in search of one lost sheep. And he cares, nurtures, protect, feed, and anoint the sheep from being biting by insects, so also God does to you, he guides you jealously from the enemies.

You are to acknowledge God as your creator with fear and trembling, love God with all your heart, spirit, and soul, serve Him and others, praise, always worship Him with thanksgiving for His unfailing love and faithfulness. You are unique talented, beautiful, worthy, important, you are special and wonderfully hand crafted for His glorious splendour.

Day 187: God wants a relationship with you, do you want a relationship with Him, like a shepherd and a sheep?

....
....
....
....
....
....
....
....
....
....
....
....

Day 188: How do you know, perceive, and understand that God made you in His image?

....
....
....
....
....
....
....

....

....

....

....

....

....

....

Day 189: Do you hear the voice of God – as a sheep hears the voice of the shepherd?

....

....

....

....

....

....

....

....

....

....

....

....

....

....

Day 190: Enter the Gates

Do you need to experience any emotions before you praise and thank God; and how do you enter God's gate or court?

....

....

....

....

....

....

....

....

....

....

....

....

....

....

....

Prayer

Thank you, Lord, that I am important to you, that you are my God, and it is you who made me. Thank you that you have placed the fullness of your beauty in my DNA, and I am fearfully and wonderfully made.

Day 191: Prayer Requests

....

....

....

....

....

....

....

....

....

....

Day 192: Meditation of Scriptures

....

....

....

....

....

....

....

....
....
....

Day 193: Reflection

....
....
....
....
....
....
....
....
....
....
....
....

Day 194: Application

How can you apply the scripture in Psalm 100: 3 to your life? Consider how it may challenge you to rely on God – note this down.

....
....
....
....

....

....

....

....

....

....

....

....

....

Day 195: Prayers Answered

....

....

....

....

....

....

....

....

....

....

....

....

....

Day 196: Gratitude

Why are you thankful? Name 5 Things for Which You are Grateful.

....
....
....
....
....
....
....
....
....
....
....
....
....
....
....
....

I am a new person in Christ (2 Corinthians 5:17)

Therefore, if anyone is in Christ [that is, grafted in, joined to Him by faith in Him as Saviour], he is a new creature [reborn and renewed by the Holy Spirit]; the old things [the previous moral and spiritual condition] have passed away. Behold, new things have come [because spiritual awakening brings a new life].

Therefore, if anyone is in Christ, he is a new creation, and all your sins are forgiven as you accept Jesus as your lord and saviour. You are no longer condemned for you have been set free by the blood of Jesus. Since your old self is gone, you no longer must worry about your past, because Jesus died for your past, present, and future. Your old nature has lost its power over you, and you are transformed into a new creation. While you were yet a sinner Christ died for you, and you are victorious in Christ Jesus.

You are the greatest manifested glory of God on earth, you are created by His glory and for His glory only. God describes you as the apple of His eye; the love of His heart; His dear children; His sons and daughters; and His dearly beloved. God's glory is in you, so do not quench that glory "God made you a little lower than the Heavenly beings and crowned you with glory and honour." (Ps. 8:5). You reflect God's magnificent glory.

According to the theologian Louis Berkhof "regeneration consist in the implanting of the principle of the new spiritual life in man, in a radical change of the governing disposition of the soul, which, under the influence of the Holy Spirit gives birth to a life that moves in a Godward direction. In principle this change affects the whole man: your intellect, will, soul, and the feelings and emotions and impact everything about who you are.

Praise God for His awesomeness. And that, by faith, you have peace with God through our Lord Jesus Christ

Day 197: How do you feel as a new creation in Christ Jesus?

....

....

....

....

....

....

....

....

....

....

....

....

Day 198: Crowned by God

Do you know that God crowned you with glory and honour, and how do you feel about being made little lower than the angel?

....

....

....

....

....

....

....

....
....
....
....
....
....
....
....

Day 199: Born of the Spirit

What do you understand by being born again and renewed by the Holy Spirit?

....
....
....
....
....
....
....
....
....
....
....
....
....
....
....
....

.

....

....

....

....

....

....

....

Milestones and celebrating commitment and Discipline.

Congratulations – You Are on Day 199!

Day 200: New In Christ

What does it mean to be in Christ and that all things become new?

....

....

....

....

....

....

....

....

....

....

....

....

....

....

....

....

....

....

....

Prayer

Thank you for making me brand new in Christ Jesus, thank you for your love, for when I was still a sinner, Christ died for me. I am grateful Lord.

Day 201: Prayer Requests

....
....
....
....
....
....
....
....
....
....

Day 202: Meditation of Scriptures

....
....
....
....
....
....
....
....

....
....
....
....
....
....
....

Day 203: Reflection

....
....
....
....
....
....
....
....
....
....
....
....
....
....
....
....
....

Day 204: Application

How do you know that you have become a new creation?

....
....
....
....
....
....
....
....
....
....
....
....
....

Day 205: Prayers Answered

....
....
....
....
....
....
....
....
....

....
....
....
....

Day 206: Gratitude

Why are you thankful? Name 5 Things for Which You are Grateful.

....
....
....
....
....
....
....
....
....
....
....
....
....

I am God's workmanship (Ephesians 2:10)

For we are His workmanship [His own master work, a work of art], created in Christ Jesus [reborn from above—spiritually transformed, renewed, ready to be used] for good works, which God prepared [for us] beforehand [taking paths which He set], so that we would walk in them [living the good life which He prearranged and made ready for us].

There are four keys in this verse to discover your purpose. Workmanship, created in Christ Jesus for good work, prepared beforehand, walk in what God had made in advance for you. "Workmanship" simply means that God handcrafted (made, manufactured, work of art, masterpiece) intricately made you for His purpose, you are uniquely one-of-a-kind bespoke created for His use, no one else on earth has your DNA. Do not copy what others are doing nor would you like to be like them. NO!!!, do not even think about conforming with your peers or the world. The whole world is waiting for your manifestation and what you have, that gift, talent, mind, and personality. One of the processes of discovering your purpose is embracing that you matter and that you are a bespoke masterpiece for such a time we are living to bring glory to God.

Day 207: What is needed so that you can become good?

....
....
....
....
....
....
....
....
....
....
....
....
....

Day 208: How do you feel to know that you were handcrafted by God for His purpose?

....
....
....
....
....
....
....
....

....

....

....

....

Day 209: What are the things that God had prepared beforehand for you?

....

....

....

....

....

....

....

....

....

....

....

....

....

Day 210: Who are you accountable to?

....

....

....

....

....
....
....
....
....
....
....
....

Day 211: What lessons can you learn from Ephesians 2:10?

....
....
....
....
....
....
....
....
....
....
....
....
....

Prayer

Thank you, Abba Father, for making me a masterpiece, thank you Lord that there is no one like me, special and uniquely me. I am grateful that no one else know me like you do.

Day 212: Prayer Requests

....
....
....
....
....
....
....
....
....
....
....
....

Day 213: Meditation of Scriptures

....
....
....
....
....
....

....
....
....
....
....
....
....
....

Day 214: Reflection

....
....
....
....
....
....
....
....
....
....
....
....
....
....
....
....
....

Day 215: Application

How do you walk in God's purpose for your life, and name 5 things?

....

....

....

....

....

....

....

....

....

....

....

....

....

Day 216: Prayers Answered

....

....

....

....

....

....

....

....

....

....
....
....
....
....

Day 217: Gratitude

Why are you thankful? Name 5 Things for Which You are Grateful.

....
....
....
....
....
....
....
....
....
....
....
....

God is with me, and I am loved by Him (Zephaniah 3:17)

The LORD your God is with you, the Mighty Warrior who saves.

He will take great delight in you; in his love he will no longer rebuke you but will rejoice over you with singing."

The Lord is reminding us here that He rejoices over His people including you with gladness and joy. Even though you walk through the valley of the shadow of death, He is with you, to protect and save you under His pavilion. As a believer, you have been saved and brought into the family of God. You may be going through hard times right now, a situation or any challenges you may be facing, know that you are not alone, God is with you, right in your midst, watching over you, working out a solution for you. The Mighty man in battle is stretching His strong and righteous arm around you.

Do not forget that the Holy Spirit dwells in you, and your body is the temple of God, so keep yourself as a living sacrifice, holy, acceptable unto God, which is your reasonable service, for His glory.

Day 218: Do you see God as a Father who is glad over His children?

....

....

....

....

....

....

....

....

....

....

....

....

Day 219: How do you feel, knowing that God is with you always?

....

....

....

....

....

....

....

....

....
....
....
....
....
....
....

Day 220: How ready are you to know God in a fresh way right Now?

....
....
....
....
....
....
....
....
....
....
....
....
....
....
....
....

Day 221: Do you know God as a might warrior, who saves, why with reasons?

....

....

....

....

....

....

....

....

....

....

....

....

....

....

....

....

....

....

Prayer

Lord thank you for the depth of your love, joy, and your salvation. Thank you, Lord, that you are always with me and my family.

Day 222: Prayer Requests

....
....
....
....
....
....
....
....
....
....
....
....

Day 223: Meditation of Scriptures

....
....
....
....
....
....
....

....
....
....
....
....
....
....

Day 224: Reflection

....
....
....
....
....
....
....
....
....
....
....
....
....
....
....

Day 225: Application

How easy is it for you that God delight In you.

....
....
....
....
....
....
....
....
....
....
....
....
....

Day 226: Prayers Answered

....
....
....
....
....
....
....
....
....

....
....
....
....

Day 227: Gratitude

Why are you thankful? Name 5 Things for Which You are Grateful.

....
....
....
....
....
....
....
....
....
....
....
....
....

I am Precious to God, honoured and God loves me (Isaiah 43:4)

Because you are precious in My sight, you are honoured and I love you, I will give other men in return for you and other peoples in exchange for your life.

God Almighty called you precious!!!! What an awesome name and a label to wear around your neck for all to see. Precious means something that is deeply treasured, truly beloved, and dear to the heart. That is who you are to God, he made you a little lower than the angels and crowned you with glory and honour. You are a child of the King of all kings, you are princes and princess. There are people who may want to demean, belittle you or discriminate against you because of who you are, do not fight or argue with them, for your distinctions are too valuable to forfeit. Enjoy who you are with the benefits that comes with who you are and whose you are.

You are precious to God and He has given you a special place of honour and loved you. That is why He is willing to trade others, to give up whole nations (everything), to save your life, for His glory. Not only are you uniquely formed, with unique makeup but you are made in His image and hidden in Christ Jesus. Don't you dare feel insecure to wear your crown of glory and honour very well for all to see and glorify your Father in heaven? You are God's beloved; He keeps pouring His love on you. Precious things are not found everywhere or with everybody but with selected few who can afford it. You are not so supposed to be with everybody or everywhere, you must act or do things intentionally because of who you are.

Day 228: How do you feel knowing that you are precious and treasured child of God?

....
....
....
....
....
....
....
....
....
....
....
....

Day 229: Do you feel honoured and loved by God?

....
....
....
....
....
....
....
....
....

....
....
....

Day 230: How have you been feeling until now that you know who you are?

....
....
....
....
....
....
....
....
....
....
....
....

Day 231: What does it mean to be a beloved of God?

....
....
....
....
....

....
....
....
....
....
....
....
....
....
....
....
....

Prayer

I am grateful Lord, that I am precious and treasured by you. Thank you for making me a little lower than the angel and that my security, self-esteem, confidence is in Christ Jesus.

Day 232: Prayer Requests

....
....
....
....
....
....
....
....
....
....

Day 233: Meditation of Scriptures

....
....
....
....
....
....
....

....
....
....
....
....
....
....

Day 234: Reflection

.

....
....
....
....
....
....
....
....
....
....
....
....
....
....

Day 235: Application

What can you learn from Isaiah 43:4 and how will it affect your self-esteem?

....
....
....
....
....
....
....
....
....
....
....
....

Day 236: Prayers Answered

....
....
....
....
....
....
....
....
....

....

....

....

....

Day 237: Gratitude

Why are you thankful? Name 5 Things for Which You are Grateful.

....

....

....

....

....

....

....

....

....

....

....

....

....

....

I am capable and self-sufficient in Christ Jesus (Philippians 4:13)

I can do all things [which He has called me to do] through Him who strengthens and empowers me [to fulfil, His purpose—I am self-sufficient in Christ's sufficiency; I am ready for anything and equal to anything through Him who infuses me with inner strength and confident peace.]

You can do all things because Jesus is your source and your strength, you cannot do anything without Jesus being the centre of it all. He is the one who gives you the ability, power, enablement, courage, and strength to do all things. Because you are made in the image of God, you dare to pursue all that God has in store for you.

Knowing who you are will liberate you, connect you to the right people, jobs, or businesses, take risks by faith, and celebrate every achievement by giving glory to God. But if you do not know who you are, the devil will rob you and kick you like a ball and you will settle for a life where you will only tolerate yourself. Your insecurity is caused by not knowing who you are. Don't you ever settle for less, you are much more, and you matter!

You are precious, treasured, honoured, a custom creation and God desires that you know who you are, and fulfil your purpose and destiny.

Day 238: Do you feel that you are incapable of doing things on own without Jesus?

....
....
....
....
....
....
....
....
....
....
....
....

Day 239: What gives you the strength to do all things and why?

....
....
....
....
....
....
....
....

....

....

....

....

....

....

....

Day 240: How has self-doubt hold you back from being capable?

....

....

....

....

....

....

....

....

....

....

....

....

....

Day 241: What is the new story God is asking you to do in view of yourself?

....
....
....
....
....
....
....
....
....
....
....
....
....
....
....

Prayer

I declare that I can do all things through Christ who strengthens me. I declare that I am who you say that I am, regardless of what people are saying, think or my past mistakes. I am Precious, honoured, capable, I am wonderful, I am chosen, I am treasured, I am royal priesthood. Thank you, Lord for everything.

Day 242: Prayer Requests

....

....

....

....

....

....

....

....

....

....

Day 243: Meditation of Scriptures

....

....

....

....

....

....

....

....

....

....

Day 244: Reflection

....

....

....

....

....

....

....

....

....

....

....

....

Day 245: Application

Consider how you can apply Philippians 4:13 to your life - explain what that looks like.

....

....

....

....

....

....

....

....

....

....

....

....

....

....

Day 246: Prayers Answered.

....

....

....

....

....

....

....

....

....

....

....

....

....

....

....

Day 247: Gratitude

Think of why you are grateful. Name Five Things for which You are Grateful.

....

....

....

....

....

....

....

....

....

....

....

....

....

....

Reflection: Shaped in my mother's womb for a specific purpose (Jeremiah 1:5):

"Before I shaped you in the womb, I knew all about you. Before you saw the light of day, I had holy plans for you: A prophet to the nations, that's what I had in mind for you."

God created and shaped you like a potter and a clay on purpose for a purpose. The Bible says before you were formed in the womb, He had holy and good plans for you to prosper, and be in health, as your soul prospers. God has carefully woven you together as a masterpiece, as an essential component in His master plan, and He uniquely fixed in you all that you need to prosper and fulfil your assignment. Your brilliance and magnificence are not meant for mediocrity or comfort zone. You have full potential waiting to be unleashed for the world to see through your multiple talents, gifts, abilities, and dreams. It is time to show the world, what you can do as a solution provider at such a time for God's glory.

Day 248: How glad are you to know that you are 'shaped for a purpose' by God?

Everything you could ever need for life and godliness has already been deposited in you by His divine power.

For all this was lavished upon you through the rich experience of knowing Jesus who has called you by name and invited you to come to Him through a glorious manifestation of his goodness. (2 Peter 1:3 TPT)

....
....
....
....
....
....
....
....
....
....
....
....
....
....
....

Day 249: Do you know your purpose and the purpose of God for your life?

....

....

....

....

....

....

....

....

....

....

....

....

Day 250: Do you know the plans of God for your life?

....

....

....

....

....

....

....

....

....

....

....

....

....

Day 251: What plans do you have for your life concerning God's calling on you?

....

....

....

....

....

....

....

....

....

....

....

....

Prayer

Thank you, Lord for shaping me in the womb for a specific purpose. Lord help, me to fulfil that purpose and to be able to walk according to your plans for my life. Thank you, for revealing who I am to me and how you have designed me for your purpose.

Day 252: Prayer Requests

....
....
....
....
....
....
....
....
....
....

Day 253: Meditation of Scriptures

....
....
....
....
....
....
....

....
....
....

Day 254: Reflection

....
....
....
....
....
....
....
....
....
....
....
....

Day 255: Application

What Are The Decisions You Have Taken Without Asking God First?

....
....
....
....
....
....

....
....
....
....
....
....
....
....

Day 256: Prayers Answered

....
....
....
....
....
....
....
....
....
....
....
....
....
....
....

Day 257: Gratitude

Why are you thankful? Name 5 Things for Which You are Grateful.

....

....

....

....

....

....

....

....

....

....

....

....

....

....

....

Reflection

I am a leader anointed, chosen, and called by God (John 15:16).

'You didn't choose me, but I've chosen and commissioned you to go into the world to bear fruit. And your fruit will last, because whatever you ask of my Father, for my sake, he will give it to you!'

An effective leader like Jesus Christ has a shared vision aligned with core values and understands what it will take to reach their team goals.

They inspire, manage, motivate, and support their teams to work creatively and confidently toward that shared vision. Also, they empower their team members to embrace their uniqueness. (Elizabeth Perry)

Everyone has the skill of being a leader because you are made in his image. God loves you so much that He desires you to be fruitful in every area of your life. Leadership is your birth right (Acts 10:34) and it is written in Genesis 1:28 that one should be fruitful. God wants you to enjoy fruitfulness, for this purpose you were created. He designed you for a special purpose, mission, and assignment. God sent you into that career, job, business, home, school, university, Church, in any area of the seven mountains of influence, to bear fruit and multiply in there.

You must remain in Christ to bear fruit because He is your source, if you are not connected to that source, you will be barren. God's superpower and your natural skills mean you are a supernatural leader as you begin to use your gifts, talents, voice, and availability to be God's representative showing love, godliness, limitless creativity, hope, gentleness, patience, endurance, and freedom in Christ. You have been anointed, chosen, and called to be a leader that leads others to salvation, into His presence and eternity. Arise and take your place NOW, you have been on this mountain (Comfort Zone) for too long.

Day 258: What does it mean to be chosen and commissioned to go into the world?

....
....
....
....
....
....
....
....
....
....
....
....
....

Day 259: What does it mean to bear fruit and in what area of your life?

....
....
....
....
....
....
....
....

....
....
....
....
....
....
....

Day 260: What does it mean to you "your fruit will last"?

....
....
....
....
....
....
....
....
....
....
....
....
....
....
....
....

Day 261: Has God ever answered your prayers and what was it?

....
....
....
....
....
....
....
....
....
....
....
....
....
....
....

Prayer

Lord Jesus, thank you for your graciousness, love, faithfulness, and compassion towards me. Lord show, me how to be a good leader and reveal my assignment and purpose to me. Thank you, Lord.

Day 262: Prayer Requests

....
....
....
....
....
....
....
....
....
....

Day 263: Meditation of Scriptures

....
....
....
....
....
....
....

....
....
....

Day 264: Reflection

....
....
....
....
....
....
....
....
....
....
....
....

Day 265: Application

What can you learn from John 15:16 and how can you apply it to yourself?

....
....
....
....
....
....

....

....

....

....

....

....

....

....

....

Day 266: Prayers Answered

....

....

....

....

....

....

....

....

....

....

....

....

....

....

Day 267: Gratitude

Why are you thankful? Name 5 Things for Which You are Grateful.

.

Accepting my Purpose

I am a warrior, Intercessor, and a watchman (2 Corinthians 10:4)

The weapons of our warfare are not physical [weapons of flesh and blood]. Our weapons are divinely powerful for the destruction of fortresses.

The battle is not yours, because as a challenge, was won by Jesus on the cross. Fear not, the Lord is your defence, protector, your covering, and you shall not be moved by any situations or circumstances of life. Because you carry something great and as an influencer impacting lives, the enemy is frightened of you and would put up a fight against you. As you try to step into your calling, there will be resistance and the enemy will *raise his ugly head* to attack you. But, but fear not, for you have overcome. God's word says: *I have told you these things, so that in Me you may have [perfect] peace. In the world, you have tribulation and distress and suffering, but be courageous [be confident, be undaunted, be filled with joy]; I have overcome the world." [My conquest is accomplished, My victory abiding.* (John 16:33)

The battle you are going through confirms that you are fearfully and wonderfully made for God's glory, you are endowed with manifold wisdom of God, imagination, and full of untapped potential inside of you. Trust God with your whole heart, have faith in Him and your ability, power, and strength in God to overcome whatever challenges come your way. You are a warrior because your heavenly Father is Jehovah man of War.

The word says:

Therefore, be strong in the Lord and the power of His might, **put on the whole armour of God**, *that you may be able to stand against the [a]wiles of the devil* (Ephesians 6:11).

Amos was a shepherd working in the field that God called him to be a watchman over in Israel. Equally, God has called you to be His *intercessor.*

Day 268: What are weapons used for and why are you a weapon in the hand of God?

....

....

....

....

....

....

....

....

....

....

....

....

....

Day 269: Why is it that the weapons of our warfare are not canal?

....

....

....

....

....

....

....

....

....

....

....

....

....

....

....

Day 270: *The battle is the Lord's.*

Why is the battle not yours and what battle are you going through right now?

....

....

....

....

....

....

....

....

....

....

....

....

....

....

Day 271: Why are we asked to put on the whole armour of God?

....
....
....
....
....
....
....
....
....
....
....
....
....
....
....
....

Prayer

Thank you, Lord for creating me in your image, as a super weapon, fully charged and equipped to defeat the enemies. Thank you for your strength, authority, anointing and my mouth given to me to declare, and speak against the enemy, so that he will flee from me.

Day 272: Prayer Requests

....

....

....

....

....

....

....

....

....

....

....

Day 273: Meditation of Scriptures

....

....

....

....

....

....

....
....
....
....
....
....

Day 274: Reflection

....
....
....
....
....
....
....
....
....
....
....
....
....
....
....
....
....
....

Day 275: Application

What is the lesson in 2 Corinthians 10:4 and how can you apply it to your life?

....
....
....
....
....
....
....
....
....
....
....
....

Day 276: Prayers Answered

....
....
....
....
....
....
....
....
....

....

....

....

....

Day 277: Gratitude

Why are you thankful? Name 5 Things for Which You are Grateful.

....

....

....

....

....

....

....

....

....

....

....

Deeper Learning: The Shepherd of the Sheep

I am a sheep of His pasture and Jesus is my Shepherd.

Know and fully recognise with gratitude that the LORD Himself is God;

It is He who has made us, [a]*not we ourselves [and we are His].*

We are His people and the sheep of His pasture. (Psalm 100: 3)

When the bible says that you are the sheep of God's pasture, it means that you acknowledge that Jesus is your Shepherd, protector, and provider, and as a shepherd care and feeds his sheep, so does Jesus care for and protect you from all evil. The sheep depend on and trust the shepherd absolutely for all its needs, so, you must trust and rely on God without doubt or leaning on your understanding. (*Trust in the LORD with all your heart and lean not on your understanding; in all your ways acknowledge him, and he will make your paths straight,* Proverbs 3:5-6)

You should acknowledge God that you will trust and be obedient to His leading and directing you into a pasture of sufficiency, where you will be fed and not lack any good thing or starved.

A pasture is a green area or place where the shepherd feeds their sheep. There is reference to green pasture in Psalm 23. It refers to a place of abundance, for the sheep to have more than enough to feed on. And this is the life of abundance, God had prepared for you, and He is calling you to live. When you accept Him as your Shepherd, Lord, and Saviour.

God is calling you into this green pasture that is plentiful, as you listen to the good shepherd, He will lead you to the pasture of His goodness and mercy, safety, grace, encouragement, love, joy, security, and peace. When you have an opportunity to be a shepherd or leader, do lead your sheep in a godly way, care for them, and direct them to the pasture of abundant life and its source, who is Jesus.

Day 278: How do you feel to be a sheep of God's pasture?

....
....
....
....
....
....
....
....
....
....
....
....
....

Day 279: Who is the good shepherd, and why did He call you His own?

....
....
....
....
....
....
....
....
....
....

....

....

....

....

....

....

Day 280: How do you describe the relationship God has with His followers? (Psalm 100:3)

....

....

....

....

....

....

....

....

....

....

....

....

....

....

....

....

....

Day 281: What do you understand by *a pasture*, and do you think that God will lead you to the pasture?

Prayer

Thank you, Lord that you are my shepherd, and I am your sheep. Help me to hear your voice, to trust you and rely on you absolutely without leaning on my own understanding. Amen.

Day 282: Prayer Requests

....

....

....

....

....

....

....

....

....

....

Day 283: Meditation of Scriptures

....

....

....

....

....

....

....

....
....
....
....
....
....
....

Day 284: Reflection

....
....
....
....
....
....
....
....
....
....
....
....
....
....
....
....
....
....

Day 285: Application

Describe the relationship that God wants to have with you and how?

....

....

....

....

....

....

....

....

....

....

....

....

Day 286: Prayers Answered

....

....

....

....

....

....

....

....

....

....
....
....
....

Day 287: Gratitude

Why are you thankful? Name 5 Things for Which You are Grateful.

....
....
....
....
....
....
....
....
....
....
....
....

Deeper Learning: Light of the World

Knowledge: I am the light of the World

"You are the light of [Christ to] the world. A city set on a hill cannot be hidden; nor does anyone light a lamp and put it under a basket, but on a lampstand, and it gives light to all who are in the house. (Mathew 5:14-15 AMP).

Because Jesus is the source of your life, you have the energy and power to shine into any form of darkness and the light will not overcome you. As the light of the world, you light up every darkness around you, no matter how small your light may be, it will always shine through darkness. When God said let your light shine before others, it means to live an active faith, not to be passive in your everyday life but to take risk as a step of faith, to fulfil your purpose. And Jesus has given you the light of divinity to fill your heart and mind, and to shine on and brighter in every area of your life. You can shine through your good works, by showing love to others, service, care, and having compassion, in the way you speak, relate, and act with others in every area of life.

No light can be hidden, and you can never be hidden as well, because of your situation, failures, challenges, or circumstances in life, and you must not allow anything to hide you. Moreover, no one puts a light under the table because a lamp is designed to serve a purpose and that is for people to see in dark places. You should place your light on the stand and use every circumstance as an opportunity to shine into darkness, for God's name to be glorified in your testimony to other. Light brightens, transform, dispels darkness, and exposes evil, and you are to enlighten the dark places in the world as God's representative.

As the light of the world, you are to shine brighter and brighter upon a perfect day like the sun, and like a diamond amongst your peers. You must never be intimated by others, fear, anxiety, worry, or depression, because the greater one is your source and He lives inside of you, so lift your head and shine for the world to see your good works and glorify your Father in Heaven.

Day 288: How do you describe yourself as the light of the world?

....

....

....

....

....

....

....

....

....

....

....

....

Day 289: Are you hiding the light that Jesus has given you and why?

....

....

....

....

....

....

....

....

....
....
....
....
....
....
....

Day 290: What does light represent; and why did Jesus call you light of the world?

....
....
....
....
....
....
....
....
....
....
....
....
....
....
....

Day 291: Why is light Said not to be hidden under the table?

....
....
....
....
....
....
....
....
....
....
....
....
....
....
....
....
....
....

Prayer

Thank you, Lord that I am the light of the world. Lord help me to continue to shine brighter and brighter upon a perfect day like the sun and Lord increase my faith amid my circumstances.

Day 292: Prayer Requests

....

....

....

....

....

....

....

....

....

....

Day 293 Meditation of Scriptures

....

....

....

....

....

....

....

....

....

....

....

....

....

....

Day 294: Reflection

....

....

....

....

....

....

....

....

....

....

....

....

....

....

....

....

....

Day 295: Application

Why is light important and how can you apply this to yourself?

....

....

....

....

....

....

....

....

....

....

....

....

....

Day 296: Prayers Answered

....

....

....

....

....

....

....

....

....

....

....

....

....

Day 297: Gratitude

Why are you thankful? Name 5 Things for Which You are Grateful.

....

....

....

....

....

....

....

....

....

....

....

....

....

I am the salt of the Earth. (Mathew 5:13)

"You are the [a]salt of the earth; but if the salt has [b]lost its taste (purpose), how can it be made salty? It is no longer good for anything, but to be thrown out and walked on by people [when the walkways are wet and slippery].

Salt is used for cooking, preservation, cleaning, and killing germs, earthworms, and ants. No other seasoning has yet been found that can satisfactorily take the place of salt. You as the salt of the earth have the same qualities as natural salt. You are to preserve lives through your prayers, encouragement, empowerment, and comfort, and by giving generously to people in need. You can drive away agents of darkness and magnetise good things into your life. (Psalm 23:6)

Who are you... who are you?

Do you know that you are the salt of the earth? Being salt means that you are to flavour the world. I must say, I do not often introduce myself as the salt of the earth nor the light of the world, I sometimes do so, when I am a guest speaker.

 What about you? Have you ever thought about it or acted like a salt or a light in darkness? Or have come across a person that has introduced themselves to you as the light of the world/salt of the earth? God knew about you before the foundation of the earth, and that is the reason why Jesus called you, the salt of the earth and the light of the world. (Mathew 5:13-14)

Just as many people came to Jesus from all walks of life, they came to listen, learn, be healed, and put their lives back together. And they came in search of meaning, direction, and purpose. You are one of those people who came to Jesus in search of meaning, direction, and purpose. You are to season and transform others' lives, which will reveal God in this generation, to help and support people to see themselves in the word of God, and through you, God will flavour and illuminate their lives.

If the salt loses its taste or savour, it is thrown away. May you not be thrown away from the Kingdom of God, you should have a unique character like salt. Its presence is not felt but its absence makes things tasteless.

"As all life on earth depends on its chemical properties to survive, so all believers depend on Jesus Christ as their source of survival." Carol Babalola.

Day 298: The Salt of the World

Why did Jesus call you the salt of the earth; what flavour can you bring to society?

....

....

....

....

....

....

....

....

....

....

....

Day 299: What are the qualities of salt and compare these to your life as a believer?

....

....

....

....

....

....

....

....

....

Day 300: How can you fulfil your calling as a salt in your job, School, business etc?

....
....
....
....
....
....
....
....
....
....
....
....
....

Day 301: How can you help to preserve truth, godliness, and goodness?

....
....
....
....
....
....
....
....

....
....
....
....
....
....
....
....
....
....
....
....
....

Prayer

Lord Jesus, thank you for calling me the salt of the earth. Lord remind me every day as your beloved child, called, equipped, and empowered to be the salt of the earth, Lord Jesus use me to preserve and transform lives. Thank you, Lord, because you will help me search for and find meaning, direction, and purpose in and for my life.

Day 302: Prayer Requests

....
....
....
....
....
....
....
....
....
....
....

Day 303: Meditation of Scriptures

....
....
....
....
....
....

....
....
....
....
....
....

Day 304: Reflection

....
....
....
....
....
....
....
....
....
....
....
....
....
....
....
....

Day 305: Application

Name some of those things that make a different and distinct in you.

....

....

....

....

....

....

....

....

....

....

....

....

Day 306: Prayers Answered

....

....

....

....

....

....

....

....

....

....

....

....

Day 307: Gratitude

Why are you thankful? Name 5 Things for Which You are Grateful.

....

....

....

....

....

....

....

....

....

....

....

....

....

....

I am peculiar, holy, and unique being unto God
(Deuteronomy 14:2)

For thou art a holy people unto the Lord thy God, and the Lord hath chosen thee to be a peculiar people unto himself, above all the nations that are upon the earth.

As a peculiar people, you are uniquely unique to God, you belong exclusively to Him, and lavishes His love upon you as His beloved child, and that is why He said He will never leave you nor forsake you. You are unusual and supernatural. God set you apart for His glory, and you were called out of billions of people on earth and chose you to be His treasured possession, a special treasure, unto Himself. Where you sold yourself for nothing, God redeemed you by His blood, because of what He has done, you are now victorious in every area of your life, powerful, an overcomer, a winner, because winners never quit and quitters never win, and you have become a leader and commander through Christ Jesus and, has made you a king to rule and reign on earth.

Moreover, God chose you to be His special possession to Himself, treasured you above all the others (nations) that are on the earth, and He wants you to be His peculiar servant, child, and worshiper, and for you to enjoy peculiar blessings, abundance, privileges, health, and wisdom. You are to behave in a special way different from others and not conform to them, compromise, or do eat the delicate of the world.

Your body is the temple of God, in which the Holy Spirit dwells, so realise that you are not of your own because you were bought at a price, therefore glorify God in your body and spirit which are God's (1 Corinthians 6:19). As a child of God, you must not mutilate (tattoo) your body and if you have cut (tattoo) in the past, all you need to do is to repent and God will forgive you as His cherished personal treasure.

Day 308: What do you understand by being peculiar people, and holy to God?

....
....
....
....
....
....
....
....
....
....
....
....
....

Day 309: Why does God want you to be Holy?

....
....
....
....
....
....
....
....

....

....

....

....

....

....

Day 310: Why did God say that your body is the temple of God; which the Holy Spirit dwells?

....

....

....

....

....

....

....

....

....

....

....

....

....

....

....

Day 311: What does Deuteronomy 14:2 mean to you?

Prayer

Thank You, Abba Father, that I am peculiar, chosen, and Holy unto you. Thank you, for the peculiar blessings, abundance, privileges, health, and wisdom, that I enjoy in Christ Jesus. Lord help, me to walk uprightly in You and to know who I am in Christ Jesus.

Day 312: Prayer Requests

....
....
....
....
....
....
....
....
....
....

Day 313: Meditation of Scriptures

....
....
....
....
....
....
....

....
....
....
....
....
....

Day 314: Reflection

....
....
....
....
....
....
....
....
....
....
....
....
....
....
....
....
....

Day 315: Application

Choose two things that you wish to sacrifice for or give up for the sake of serving God?

....
....
....
....
....
....
....
....
....
....
....
....

Day 316: Prayers Answered

....
....
....
....
....
....
....
....
....

....
....
....
....

Day 317: Gratitude

Why are you thankful? Name 5 Things for Which You are Grateful.

....
....
....
....
....
....
....
....
....
....
....
....

I am forgiven by God (1 john 1:9 AMP)

If we [freely] admit that we have sinned and confess our sins, He is faithful and just [true to His own nature and promises] and will forgive our sins and cleanse us continually from all unrighteousness [our wrongdoing, everything not in conformity with His will and purpose].

The Bible says that if you confess your sins, God is faithful and just to forgive you of your sin and purify you from all unrighteousness. God is just, when He forgives you of your sins, He cleanses you of all your trespasses as if you have never done wrong, and then you start on a clean slate. After the man had sinned and come short of the glory of God, He sent His only begotten son in a human form to die on the cross for you and me.

This same Jesus who died on the cross for your sin came to reconcile you back to God. After you receive Jesus as your Lord and Saviour, you become a new creation in Christ Jesus, and your sins have been forgiven. Jesus selflessly came to the world and paid the price for our sins became an example and taught us how to love God the Father with all our heart, spirit, soul, and body and the second one is like it, to love our neighbours as ourselves.

We all have sinned and have come short of the glory of God. The book of proverbs asked this question, who can say,

"I have made my heart clean, I am pure from sin"? (Proverbs 20:9)

No one is perfect without sin, but the bible admonishes us to walk in holiness, faultlessness in motives and thoughts and righteousness in moral actions because of sin, we all need Jesus as our Saviour, whosoever we obey, we become a slave to that.

To ponder: Whenever, you are struggling with sins, ask the Holy Spirit to help you, come to God with a contrite heart and ask for repentance and forgiveness. As you walk in the light, this will constantly remind you of your sins and to avoid sinning. Perhaps you make a mistake or failure, do not give up or sit there on the dirt, please find your way back to God and ask for His forgiveness and you Must not allow man to judge or condemn you, for the grace of God is sufficient for you.

And if you are struggling with sin, it does not mean you lack faith, but God is faithful and just to forgive you of your sins if you turn to Him in repentance and ask for forgiveness, He will surely forgive you because, contrite and broken hearts God will not despise. God is looking for those with yielded, broken, and contrite heart because your yielded heart is your sacrifice to God.

The fountain of your pleasure is found in the sacrifice of my shattered heart before you. You will not despise my tenderness as I humbly bow down at your feet (Psalm 51:6TPT).

If anyone was to take vengeance, it would have been Jesus but rather He said on the cross, *Father, forgive them, for they do not know what they are doing.* Wow!!! Lord, have mercy on us.

Day 318: What is your attitude towards sin in your life?

....
....
....
....
....
....
....
....
....
....
....
....

Day 319: What is the plan of God for your life?

....
....
....
....
....
....
....
....
....
....

Day 320: Do you believe in the forgiveness of God?

....
....
....
....
....
....
....
....
....
....
....
....

Day 321: What price did Jesus pay for your sin?

....
....
....
....
....
....
....
....
....
....

Prayer

Lord Jesus, thank you for the price you paid for my sins, to reconcile me back to God.

Lord, I surrender all to you today, help me to have a yielded, contrite, and broken heart and walk with the Holy Spirit. May your grace be sufficient for me.

Day 322: Prayer Requests

....
....
....
....
....
....
....
....
....
....
....

Day 323: Meditation of scriptures

....
....
....
....
....
....
....

....
....
....
....
....
....
....

Day 324: Reflection

....
....
....
....
....
....
....
....
....
....
....
....
....
....
....
....

Day 325: Application

How do you have a contrite and broken heart?

....

....

....

....

....

....

....

....

....

....

....

....

Day 326: Prayers Answered

....

....

....

....

....

....

....

....

....

....

....

....

Day 327: Gratitude

Why are you thankful? Name 5 Things for Which You are Grateful.

....

....

....

....

....

....

....

....

....

....

....

....

I am the temple of the Lord and Holy Spirit lives inside of me (1 Corinthians 6:19-20 NLT)

Don't you realise that your body is the temple of the Holy Spirit, who lives in you and was given to you by God? You do not belong to yourself, for God bought you with a high price. So, you must honour God with your body.

This question asked, needed an affirmative answer, because ignorance is not an excuse in the court of law, but also in the court of heaven. As believers, we are told in the bible repeatedly that our bodies do not belong to us but to God.

See, He created you in His image and Jesus bought you with a high price by the shedding of His blood on the cross for you, to reconcile you back to God. Your body does not belong to you, it was given to you as a gift from God and you are to take care of it, spiritually, physically, and your wellbeing. When you begin to separate your body from the Holy Spirit and look at yourself that you are too small to carry out God's plan for your life, then you start having problems with low self-esteem and poor self-worth. Life is not about the container but the content inside of it, because He that is in you is greater than that in the world. God sanctified your body and set you apart for His glory, so do not abuse your body with substances, drugs, tattoos, alcoholism, or sexual abuse. We are encouraged to manage ourselves and stop anger, bitterness, resentment, jealousy, anxiety, and unforgiveness. If you do not forgive others, God will not forgive you of your sins. Please avoid sexual sins. No other sin affects the body in as negatively and long-lasting manner as this does. For sexual immorality is a sin against your own body, but the one who is joined to the Lord is one spirit with Him. Your body is a dwelling place for the Holy Spirit, which is sacred to him as a temple, which must not be defiled by the sin of fornication or adultery. You are a vessel, and you must preserve it for God's glory.

Paul sternly pointed out that what believers intimately do with their bodies affects the spiritual state of their soul, this is the case with sexual sin. The one flesh union of marital sex reflects realities about God. Sexual activity outside of this context violates the image that God has stamped into our psyches and even into our bodies as male and female.

If you burn within yourself and you are of age, get married, and stop sleeping around with different people, as you sleep with anyone, you are sharing part of yourself with that person.

Day 328: Do you know that your body is the temple of God?

....
....
....
....
....
....
....
....
....
....
....
....

Day 329: What is a temple and why does the Holy Spirit dwell inside of you?

....
....
....
....
....
....
....
....
....

....
....
....
....
....
....
....

Day 330: Why are you not allowed to commit sexual sin?

....
....
....
....
....
....
....
....
....
....
....
....
....
....
....
....

Day 331: Union in One Flesh

What does it : *'one flesh union' in marital sex mean in* reflecting realities about God?

....

....

....

....

....

....

....

....

....

....

....

....

....

....

....

....

.....

Prayer

Lord thank you, for making my body to be the temple in which the Holy Spirit dwells.

Lord, help me to make my body a living sacrifice, pleasing unto you Lord.

Day 332: Prayer Requests

....
....
....
....
....
....
....
....
....
....

Day 333: Meditation of Scriptures

....
....
....
....
....
....
....
....

....

....

....

....

....

....

Day 334: Reflection

....

....

....

....

....

....

....

....

....

....

....

....

....

....

....

Day 335: Application

What does it mean that you *were bought* with a price?

....
....
....
....
....
....
....
....
....
....
....
....

Day 336: Prayers Answered

....
....
....
....
....
....
....
....
....

....

....

....

....

....

Day 337: Gratitude

Why are you thankful? Name 5 Things for Which You are Grateful.

....

....

....

....

....

....

....

....

....

....

....

....

....

I am more than a conqueror and I am an overcomer (Romans 8:37)

Yet in all these things we are more than conquerors and gain an overwhelming victory through Him who loved us [so much that He died for us].

You are more than a conqueror because Jesus fought and won the battle for you. In this life, there is so many ups and downs, tribulations, challenges, issues and yes overwhelming circumstance, life can be very hard for some people, but even when you fail, fall, or mess up, know that God is with you because he said he will leave you nor forsake you even in times of trouble, He is with you. You are more than a conqueror, not of your strength nor power but through Christ who loved you with everlasting love.

'John Gill's Exposition of the Bible tells us that *not only do we have victory over sin and Satan, but over the world, afflictions, and persecutions in it. But not only overcome but better off and stronger for it!*"

Your mind is like a battlefield where you have to put up a fight against failure. It is become a conqueror and overcomer. It is a place where you live in victory. So be careful that you are not defeated in your mind before the battle starts but meditate on these things, that are pure, noble, excellent, of good report, peaceful, joyful, favour, lovely, virtuous, and anything of praiseworthy; that will make your faith and joy to increase. only then will you conquer with victory over sin, Satan and the world of afflictions, persecutions, pains, sickness, and weaknesses.

"I have told you these things, so that in Me you may have [perfect] peace. In the world, you have tribulation and distress and suffering, but be courageous [be confident, be undaunted, be filled with joy]; I have overcome the world." [My conquest is accomplished,

My victory abiding."] John 16:33.

And God's demonstrated love is our glorious victory over all things.

On the journey to success, you will fall several times, fail, be misunderstood, and denied of many things by others, or you may have a disability, and make mistakes, but you overcame by the blood of Jesus who gave you victory, and you will become more victorious when God turns your life experiences for His good works.

Day 338: How do you know that you are an overcomer?

....
....
....
....
....
....
....
....
....
....
....

Day 339: Who are the conquerors and why?

....
....
....
....
....
....
....
....
....
....
....

Day 340: How do you feel being a conqueror without fighting a battle?

....
....
....
....
....
....
....
....
....

Day 341: Why is your mind a battlefield and what can you do about this?

....
....
....
....
....
....
....
....
....

Prayer

I am so grateful Abba Father for my victory in Christ Jesus. Thank you, for making me a conqueror and an overcome in every area of my life.

Day 342: Prayer Requests

....
....
....
....
....
....
....
....
....
....

Day 343: Meditation of Scriptures

....
....
....
....
....
....
....
....

....

....

....

....

....

....

Day 344: Reflection

....

....

....

....

....

....

....

....

....

....

....

....

....

....

....

....

Day 345: Application

What does Jesus mean that he has "overcome" the world; please consider with examples?

....
....
.
....
....
....
....
....
....
....
....
....
....
....

Day 346: Prayers Answered

....
....
....
....
....
....

....

....

....

....

....

....

....

Day 347: Gratitude

Why are you thankful? Name 5 Things for Which You are Grateful.

....

....

....

....

....

....

....

....

....

....

....

A Birth Right to Blessings

I am blessed and I have the right to be blessed (Ephesians 1:3, & Numbers 36:10-12 NLT)

'All praise to God, the Father of our Lord Jesus Christ, who has blessed us with every spiritual blessing in the heavenly realms because we are united with Christ.'

All things have been given to you because of Jesus Christ, everything you need to live on earth, power, grace, wisdom, knowledge, understanding, money, and good health. You have the right to be blessed as God has endowed you with the ability or power to make wealth. Every day is a gift from God and what you do on the day with your talent is a gift to God. Are you hiding your talent because someone has said negative things about it? Stereotype, Whatever the excuses, you are limited by your creativity, imagination, and concentration. Do not suppress your God-given ability, trying to live up to some negative stereotype. He paid a price for your inheritance; it caused the Father the Son's life and that is what you are rejecting to accept His inheritance.

The daughters of Zelophehad challenged the system at a time when women were considered inferior to men. (Numbers 27:4-8) despite public opinion, they asked for their rights, and they got what they wanted, a closed mouth is a closed heaven, if they had not opened their mouth, they would not have gotten their right. The daughters of Zelophehad became the pacesetters and changed the policy or law of the land for one single act, would you do the same today, to get all that belongs to you?

Some of you are living a frustrated, boring life because you have not challenged life, you need to unleash your potential, release yourself, and begin to use your talents and gifts for God's glory. Do not construct obstacles in your mind, and not be limited to settling for less. Arise!!! Shine for God's glory, if the daughter of Zelophehad asked for their rights and it was granted although, it took a while, God will surely grant your request now. Ask and you shall receive.

Day 348: Do you know that you are blessed by God?

....
....
....
....
....
....
....
....
....
....
....
....

Day 349: Are you using your talents and gifts to glorify God?

....
....
....
....
....
....
....
....
....
....

Day 350: What rights have you in Christ Jesus?

....
....
....
....
....
....
....
....
....
....
....
....

Day 351: In which area of your life, are you hiding your talents and gift?

....
....
....
....
....
....
....
....
....

....
....
....
....
....
....
....
....
....

Prayer

Thank you, Lord, that you have freely given to me every spiritual blessing in heavenly place and thank you for the rights that I have in Christ Jesus.

Day 352: Prayer Requests

....
....
....
....
....
....
....
....
....
....

Day 353: Meditation of Scriptures

....
....
....
....
....
....
....
....

....
....
....
....
....
....
....

Day 354: Reflection

....
....
....
....
....
....
....
....
....
....
....
....
....
....
....

Day 355: Application

What is a spiritual blessing (Ephesians 1:3) and how do you apply it to yourself?

....
....
....
....
....
....
....
....
....
....
....
....

Day 356: Gratitude

Why are you thankful? Name 5 Things for Which You are Grateful.

....
....
....
....
....
....
....
....

....

....

....

....

....

....

....

....

....

....

....

Deeper Learning: Created in God's image – I am Good Enough

I am a good thing, and I am somebody excellent (Genesis 1: 27 AMP)

So God created human beings[a] in his own image. In the image of God, he created them; male and female he created them.

When God looked over eternity, He saw you, everything He had created, and those things that he would create around and for you. He saw your past, present, and future, and your full traits, personality, and abilities that you would need to complete His purpose for your life, He chose the environment, family, and destiny helpers that will be necessary for you to develop your gifts and talents, that He has given to you.

After all, He had created, He looked at you and said, "This is good" and very good".

Question : Do you have the same opinion about yourself, and you do agree with God's opinion about you?

You must appreciate who you are, whose you are and the way you are created by God because others will treat you the way, you treat and respect yourself. If you are attracting people who do not love, respect, and treat you right, you are to be blamed because there is a signal you are sending to them to treat you as such.

You can change that from today, by accepting who you are as a royal priesthood, heir to God, walking majestically as a prince or princess of the Most-High, just like Prince Williams of the United Kingdom, or being bold like a lion, who walks fearlessly in the bush knowing fully well that he is the king of the animals.

You can change that negative vibe to positive vibes, by lifting your shoulders, and declaring that I am a good thing, I am somebody excellent, I am fearfully and wonderfully made, I am a masterpiece, God's special treasure and a temple of the Holy Spirit, by saying these, your spirit will exude your presence with others. When you walk into a room, your quality of inner strength will make you attractive, and cause others to recognise and pay attention to you, because your character is now magnetic, projecting your self-esteem and the power of God's Spirit within you.

Prayer

Lord I am grateful for making me in your own image and calling me good. Thank you for who you have made me to be and that in you I live, move, and have my being. Thank you that I am somebody great, valued and very important to my generation.

Day 357: Why did God look at *you* and say, "This is very good?"

....
....
....
....
....
....
....
....
....
....

Day 358: Can you explain why God loved you so much, that He created and gave you all things that you needed in life?

....
....
....
....
....

....
....
....
....
....
....
....
....

Day 359: How do you feel, by knowing that you are created in God's image?

....
....
....
....
....
....
....
....
....
....
....
....
....
....
....

Day 360: Why do you need to appreciate and love yourself?

....
....
....
....
....
....
....
....
....
....

Day 361: Prayer Requests

....
....
....
....
....
....
....
....
....
....
....

Day 362: Meditation of Scriptures

....
....
....
....
....
....
....
....
....
....
....
....

Day 363: Reflection

....
....
....
....
....
....
....
....
....
....

Day 364: Application

How do you appreciate yourself and increase self-esteem?

....
....
....
....
....
....
....
....
....
....
....
....

Day 365: Prayers Answered

....
....
....
....
....
....
....
....
....

....

....

....

....

Day 366: Gratitude & Reflections of 365 Days of Knowing Who You Are in Christ

Consider Why you are grateful, after this journey of deeper learning this year?

List a few things for which you are grateful, having completed this personal discovery:

....

....

....

....

....

....

....

....

....

....

....

Review

Establishing Foundations – through Self-Esteem

Introduction to Nurturing a Healthy You

Self-esteem plays a crucial role in our overall well-being and happiness. It is the way individuals perceive and value themselves, impacting our thoughts, emotions, and actions. Nurturing a healthy sense of self-esteem is essential for personal growth, resilience, and a positive outlook on life. Poor self-esteem (bad, condemning feelings about yourself) are weight that keeps believers under condemnation and causes them to be less than what God intends. Believers are to combat such feelings of inferiority (Hebrew 12:1).

Proper self-esteem in a follower of Christ is a matter of recognising and confronting yourself in your humanity, including the tendency to sin, "going astray" (1 Peter 2:25). it is also a matter of embracing Jesus' work on the cross, His grace that covers a multitude of sins.

The process of comprehending God's infinite care for the individual, each with unique strengths and weaknesses, puts a perspective on self-esteem, psalm 139 expresses the wonder of being uniquely created by God, and the intimate care of his presence always. Jesus tenderly described his love for his children in (Matthew 6:25-34)

Your self-worth, self-esteem or personal significance is the same and it is characterised by a quiet sense of self-respect and a feeling of satisfaction with who you are. True self-worth is not a pride based on an evaluation of your performance. Or opinions of others You have got absolutely nothing to do with your self-worth or significance, it is all about God who created you in His image and made you complete in Christ Jesus. Are you glad, that you, are you? If you are not, you might think that you would be happier if you could perform like someone else.

Do you feel you have a healthy sense of self-worth? This is not a neutral feeling about yourself but a prevailing sense of value that is not related to your performance. A healthy self-concept is the recognition of one's value and worth the understanding that as a unique human being, no one has certain gifts and abilities unlike anyone else and can contribute to the world in a special way. Success is both pleasant and encouraging but it is the by-product of stability not self-esteem.

The prerequisites to healthy self-esteem and strategies for cultivating a healthy self-image include:

- ❖ Recognise the need of a saviour Isaiah 53 :6
- ❖ Accepting being in the beloved Ephesians 1:6, Romans 8: 1
- ❖ Move forward in God's plan for your life Philippines 3:13-14
- ❖ Have a realistic view of yourself Romans 12:3
- ❖ Avoid comparison to others 2Corinthians 10:12

A person with healthy self-esteem is marked by these characteristics.

- ❖ Resting in "Ownership" by God (1Corinthian 3:16)
- ❖ Submitting to being the workmanship of God (Ephesians 2:10)
- ❖ Appreciating the difference of orders, (1 Corinthians 10:12:1-31)
- ❖ Willingness to take risks, step of faith (Esther 4:13-16)
- ❖ Forging good relationships with others (Ruth 1 :16-17)

God does not evaluate human worth as we do. He looks to the heart within, while we tend to look only at the outer frame (1 Sam.16 :7, 1 Peter 3 :3- 4.) The heart of a healthy self-esteem is recognising that self must be seen as created for God's glory. We might more accurately say that within every believer there must be God's esteem, which accepts whatever lot in life is ours.

We must be willing to change weaknesses into strength when possible, and when that is not possible, we are to look for opportunities for God to be glorified even in our failures and suffering. God does not make mistakes and He is never finished working in us as we continue to refine and edify, helping each other to reach our maximum potential (1peter 5:10).

Negatives can be changed into positives and tragedies can transform you into a better person.

1. Understanding Self-Esteem

To cultivate a healthy sense of self-esteem, it is important to understand what it entails. Self-esteem is the evaluation we make about ourselves, encompassing our beliefs, self-worth, and self-confidence. It affects how we perceive our capabilities and how we respond to challenges. By recognizing the components of self-esteem, we can begin to develop a healthier perspective.

2. Identifying and Challenging Negative Self-Talk

Negative self-talk can significantly impact our self-esteem. The internal dialogue we have with ourselves often shapes our beliefs about our abilities and worth. Identifying negative thought patterns and replacing them with positive and supportive self-talk allows us to shift our mindset and nurture a healthier self-image.

3. Celebrating Strengths and Acknowledging Achievements

Recognising our strengths and accomplishments is vital for building self-esteem. By focusing on our unique talents, gifts, skills, and achievements, we can develop a positive perception of ourselves. Setting realistic goals and celebrating every small victory along the way boosts self-confidence and reinforces a healthy self-esteem.

4. Cultivating Self-Compassion and Acceptance

Developing self-compassion and acceptance is essential in nurturing a healthy self-esteem. Embracing both our strengths and our perceived flaws with kindness and understanding allows us to appreciate our individuality. Practicing self-care, engaging in self-reflection, and being mindful of our needs contribute to developing self-compassion and acceptance.

5. Surrounding Yourself with Positive Influences

Our environment and the people we surround ourselves with have a significant impact on our self-esteem. Surrounding ourselves with positive, supportive, and encouraging individuals who uplift and value us enhances our self-worth and belief in ourselves. Establishing healthy boundaries and distancing ourselves from toxic relationships or negative influences is crucial for preserving and building our self-esteem.

6. Seeking Personal Growth and Learning

Continuous personal growth and learning contribute to our self-esteem. Engaging in activities that expand our knowledge, skills, or hobbies boosts self-confidence and fosters a sense of accomplishment. Embracing new challenges and learning from failures encourages resilience and a positive self-perception.

Conclusion

Cultivating a healthy sense of self-esteem is an ongoing journey that requires self-reflection, **self-compassion**, and a commitment to personal growth. By understanding the components **of self-esteem,** challenging negative self-talk, celebrating strengths and achievements, practicing self-compassion, cultivating positive influences, and seeking personal growth, we nurture and maintain a healthy self-image. Remember, building self-esteem is not about comparing ourselves to others, but about embracing our uniqueness and valuing ourselves for who we truly are as a masterpiece, carefully handcrafted by God for His purpose. These are assurances of God's love which can build one up in their personal journey. Ponder on them!

Memorise And Meditate On These Scriptures

Warnings for Believers

Do not reject Christ' superiority	Hebrews 1:1-4
Do not neglect your salvation	Hebrews 2:1-4
Do not reject Christ	Hebrews 3:7-15
Do not fail to enter Christ's rest	Hebrews 4:11-13
Do not sin wilfully	Hebrews 10:26-31
Do not reject God's grace	Hebrews 12:14-17
Do not reject the heavenly voice	Hebrews 12:25-29

The Answers to Inappropriate Anger

Do not give full vent to your anger	Proverbs 29:11
Do not revenge on a violator	Romans 12:19
Do not get caught up in name calling	Mathew 5: 22
Do not expect perfection from people	Romans 3:10, 23
Seek out the source of your anger	Psalms 139: 23-24
Ask your wise God for His wisdom	James 1: 5
Be slow to speak if angry	James 1:19-20
Release your right to stay angry	Colossians 3: 8
Give your anger to God	1 Peter 5: 7
Pray for those who persecute you	Mathew 5: 44
Forgive as the Lord forgave you	Colossians 3: 13
Trust God to bring good from your trials	Romans 8: 28
Stay ready to forgive anyone for anything	Ephesians 4:31-32

Pray: Lord, I see that anger is one little letter away from Danger. Lord help me and deliver me from the spirit of anger.

GOD ANSWERS TO DIFFICULT QUESTIONS

YOUR QUESTION	HIS ANSWER
Where was God when this happened to me?	He was there, He sees everything (Prov. 15:3)
Didn't He care?	Yes, He did and still does (Nah1:7,1Pet.5:6)
How could a loving God allow this to happen?	God gave us freedom of choice (Deut.30:15-20)
Does the Lord Understand how I feel?	Yes, more than anyone (Is.53:3,Heb.4:15)
Is recovery possible?	With God all things are possible (Math.19:26, Jer. 17:14)
How can I be healed?	Trust God to be faithful to His word (Ps.18:25)
Where do I begin?	God hears you, confess your hurt Ps. 34:17-18,
	Give your hurt to Him (1 Pet. 5:7)
	Forgive the one who has grieved you (Col. 3:13)
Isn't forgiveness difficult?	Yes, but what God commands you to do, He will equip you to do (1 Thess.5:24)
	realise that God has forgiven you (Eph. 4:22)
Then what do I do?	Do not take revenge, God will deal with the violator, (Rom. 8:28)

Let go and move on with life (Is. 43:18-19)

Look for the good that will come out of the bad (Rom. 8:28)

When will I heal?

Healing of deep hurt it takes time (Eccl. 3:3)

It is a process of facing the harm (Ps. 51:6)

Acknowledging your feelings (Eccl. 3:4-8)

Applying God's truth from His Word (Ps. 107:20)

Listen for God's Replies

When you want to live life successfully	Romans 12:1-2
When enjoyment seems too important	Galatians 5:1-26
When you want inward peace	Romans 8:12-39
When you feel discouraged	Psalm 23: 42
When friends are unfaithful	1 Corinthians 13:1-13
When tempted to do wrong	Psalm19: 1-14
When you seem too busy	Eccles 3:1-15
When a crisis comes	Job 28: 10-28
When you are jealous	James 3:1-12
When you are impatient	Psalm 40:1-17
When you are bored and confused	Psalm 103
When you have a grudge	2 Corinthians 4: 1-18
When you are disobedient	Luke 5:1-11
When your faith is weak	Psalm 146
When God seems far away	Psalm 25

Get The Wisdom of God

Wisdom is the only thing that you need, to be successful and maintain it. The bible encourages us to get wisdom at all costs, in Proverbs 4: 5-9: *"Get wisdom! Get understanding! Do not forget, nor turn away from the words of my mouth. Do not forsake her, and she will preserve you; Love her, and she will keep you. Wisdom is the principal thing; Therefore, get wisdom. And in all your getting, get understanding. Exalt her, and she will promote you; She will bring you honour, when you embrace her.*

She will place on your head an ornament of grace; A crown of glory she will deliver to you."

The book of James emphasises that anyone who lacks wisdom, should ask God for it, and He gives it out generously to all:

If any of you lacks wisdom [to guide him through a decision or circumstance], he is to ask of [our benevolent] God, who gives to everyone generously and without rebuke or blame, and it will be given to him.

Two forms of wisdom regulate our lives, identified as worldly and spiritual.

Worldly wisdom

Sees the message of the cross as foolishness	1 Corinthians 1: 18
Does not know God	1 Corinthians 1: 21
Boast in men	1 Corinthians 3: 21
Takes pride in human knowledge	1 Corinthians 8: 2
It is 'puffed up'	1 Corinthians 4: 6
Criticises leadership	1 Corinthians 4: 8
Relies on the power of words	1 Corinthians 4:20

Takes pride in personal accomplishments	1 Corinthians 4: 7
Scoffs at differences	1 Corinthians 12: 21
Insists on personal rights	1 Corinthians 8: 9
Is insensitive to others	1 Corinthians 8: 11
Arrogantly wounds others	1 Corinthians 8: 12
Leads to envy, strife, and division	1 Corinthians 1: 10,33
Is full of malice	1 Corinthians 14: 20
Is subject to fall	1 Corinthians 10: 12
Is often caught in its own craftiness	1 Corinthians 3: 19
Shows immature understanding	1 Corinthians 13:11-12
Will not last	1 Corinthians 3:15

Spiritual Wisdom of God

Realising the message of the cross is the power of God	1 Corinthians 1:18
Demonstrates the power of God	1 Corinthians 2:5
Glories in the Lord	1 Corinthians 1:31
Knows the mind of Christ	1 Corinthians 2:16
Seeks meekness and humility	1 Corinthians 2:3
Submits to Spiritual Leadership	1 Corinthians14:37,16:16
Relies on the power of God	1 Corinthians 4:20
Recognises God as source of everything	1 Corinthians 6:19-20
Respects diversity	1 Corinthians 12:11
Becomes servant of God and of all	1 Corinthians 9:19
Edifies others	1 Corinthians 8:1
Seeks another's well-being	1 Corinthians10: 24

Pursues unity	1 Corinthians 12:13
Walk in the way of love	1 Corinthians 13:1
Stands up under temptation	1 Corinthians 10:13
Maintains self-control and discipline	1 Corinthians 6:12,9:27
Develops maturity	1 Corinthians 2:6
Will last	1 Corinthians 3:10-14

More books written by Carol Babalola are as follows.
Find them on Amazon.

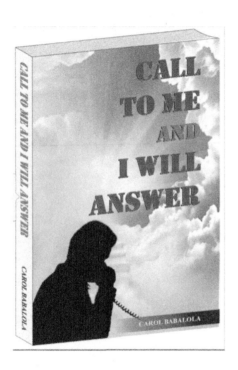

"We are all sent into the world for a purpose and to make an impact, so the neglect of our assignment will lead to living defeated and unfulfilled lives.' Who are you?"

"Knowing who you are and your identity in Christ Jesus is crtical to the fulfilment

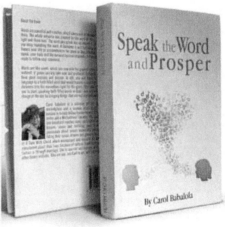

Index

- Greene, L., & Burke, G. (2007). Beyond self-actualization. *Journal of Health and Human Services Administration*, 116-128.

- Krems, J. A., Kenrick, D. T., & Neel, R. (2017). Individual perceptions of self-actualization: What functional motives are linked to fulfilling one's full potential?. *Personality and Social Psychology Bulletin, 43*(9), 1337-1352.

- See the diagram below,
- https://www.berkeleywellbeing.com/self-actualization.html

- The triangle covenant,
- https://www.google.com/search?q=triangle+about+god&sca_esv=570134643&rlz=1C5CHFA_enGB748GB748&sxsrf=AM9HkKm7wFvwv9QUKqSMBhVuX_Ycpu45HA%3A16

- https://i.ytimg.com/vi/KfAoBIGo Os/maxresdefault.jpg

- https://bible-truth-zone.blogspot.com/2014/05/
- https://lovefirstcoast.org/23124-2/

- https://eu.theleafchronicle.com/story/life/faith/2014/10/17/message-week-ten-steps-toward-finding-wholeness/17455649/#:~:text=Psalm%2073%3A26%20reads%2C%20%E2%80%9C,are%20not%20complete%20without%20him.
- **Faith Outreach Community Church**, Pastors David, and Barbara Wesner, 1235 Northfield Drive, near Exit 1

- https://www.ernestangley.org/read/article/we_are_complete_in_jesus2#:~:text=To%20be%20complete%20is%20to,set%20us%20free%20from%20sin. Ernest Angley Ministry

- Significance of Sonship: Adoption as a Child of God
- **Darrell W. Wood**
- **Retired Chaplain at Hendrick Medical Center.**
- Published Jun 23, 2021
- The search for significance by Robert S. McGee (adapted)

Printed in Great Britain
by Amazon